Becoming a

COUPLE

of Promise

BY THE
AUTHOR
OF THE BEST
SELLING BOOK
"SEX BEGINS
IN THE
KITCHEN"

DR. KEVIN LEMAN

NAVPRESS
BRINGING TRUTH TO LIFE
P.O. Box 35001, Colorado Springs, Colorado 80935

OUR GUARANTEE TO YOU

We believe so strongly in the message of our books that we are making this quality guarantee to you. If for any reason you are disappointed with the content of this book, return the title page to us with your name and address and we will refund to you the list price of the book. To help us serve you better, please briefly describe why you were disappointed. Mail your refund request to: NavPress, P.O. Box 35002, Colorado Springs, CO 80935.

I wish to express my thanks to friends Dan and Leslie Chaverin for permission to use material from their Marriage Enrichment Course of the North Way Family Institute. You'll find this material, in adapted form, in several of the "Note-it" sidebars. For more information about the institute, call (520) 797-3830.

The Navigators is an international Christian organization. Our mission is to reach, disciple, and equip people to know Christ and to make Him known through successive generations. We envision multitudes of diverse people in the United States and every other nation who have a passionate love for Christ, live a lifestyle of sharing Christ's love, and multiply spiritual laborers among those without Christ.

NavPress is the publishing ministry of The Navigators. NavPress publications help believers learn biblical truth and apply what they learn to their lives and ministries. Our mission is to stimulate spiritual formation among our readers.

Cover illustration by Bonnie Reiser

Some of the anecdotal illustrations in this book are true to life and are included with the permission of the persons involved. All other illustrations are composites of real situations, and any resemblance to people living or dead is coincidental.

Unless otherwise identified, all Scripture quotations in this publication are taken from the *HOLY BIBLE: NEW INTERNATIONAL VERSION* ® (NIV®). Copyright © 1973, 1978, 1984 by International Bible Society. Used by permission of Zondervan Publishing House. All rights reserved. Other versions used include *The Living Bible* (TLB), copyright 1971, used by permission of Tyndale House Publishers, Inc., Wheaton, IL 60189, all rights reserved; and the *King James Version* (KJV).

Printed in the United States of America

1 2 3 4 5 6 7 8 9 10 11 12 13 14 15 / 05 04 03 02 01 00 99

FOR A FREE CATALOG OF
NAVPRESS BOOKS & BIBLE STUDIES,
CALL 1-800-366-7788 (USA)
OR 1-416-499-4615 (CANADA)

This book is affectionately dedicated to Kristin Leman O'Reilly and her husband, Dennis O'Reilly, who were married on March 27, 1999; and to Holly Leman Campbell and her husband, Andrew Campbell, who were married on July 24, 1999. May the truths that are in this book be lived out in your lives as you enjoy the beauty of growing together as one in Christ. I love you very much. May God richly bless you and keep you close to Him.

Contents

Introduction 11

Session 1
The Original Designer Genes 17

Session 2
Build It Right, Build It Strong 39

Session 3
The Submission Mission 59

Session 4
"What's Wrong?" "Nothing!" 77

Session 5
Her Needs and His 95

Session 6
Affairproof Your Marriage! 115

Session 7
A Marriage That's Great for Your Kids 133

Session 8
Stepfamilies Don't Blend . . . They Collide! 153

Resources

The topics we'll tackle in this study guide are developed more fully in several of my previous books. It would be great to have copies of these available for those who want to explore a topic in greater detail.

The New Birth Order Book (Grand Rapids, Mich.: Revell, 1998).

Sex Begins in the Kitchen (Grand Rapids, Mich: Revell, 1999).

Women Who Try Too Hard (Grand Rapids, Mich.: Revell, 1998).

When Your Best Is Not Good Enough (Grand Rapids, Mich.: Revell, 1997).

Keeping Your Family Together When the World Is Falling Apart (Colorado Springs, Colo.: Focus on the Family, 1993).

The 6 Stress Points in a Woman's Life (Grand Rapids, Mich.: Revell, 1999).

Living in a Stepfamily Without Getting Stepped On (Nashville, Tenn.: Nelson, 1994).

Making Children Mind Without Losing Yours (Grand Rapids, Mich.: Revell, 1984).

Becoming the Parent God Wants You to Be (Colorado Springs, Colo.: NavPress, 1998).

What a Difference a Daddy Makes (Nashville, Tenn.: Nelson, 1999).

The topics we'll tackle in this study guide are developed more fully in my previous books. It would be great to have copies of these available for those who want to explore a topic in further detail. If you are unable to find these resources in your local bookstore, please call 1-800-770-3830 for orders only.

Sex Begins in the Kitchen
Grand Rapids, Mich.: Revell, 1984.

Keeping Your Family Together When the World Is Falling Apart
Colorado Springs, Colo.: Focus on the Family, 1993.

The New Birth Order Book
Grand Rapids, Mich.: Revell, 1998.

Living in a Stepfamily Without Getting Stepped On
Nashville, Tenn.: Nelson, 1994.

Bringing Up Kids Without Tearing Them Down
Nashville, Tenn.: Nelson, 1995.

Making Children Mind Without Losing Yours
Grand Rapids, Mich.: Revell, 1984.

Becoming the Parent God Wants You to Be
Colorado Springs, Colo.: NavPress, 1998.

What a Difference a Daddy Makes
Nashville, Tenn.: Nelson, 1999.

Winning the Rat Race
Nashville, Tenn.: Nelson, 1996.

The 6 Stress Points in a Woman's Life
Grand Rapids, Mich.: Revell, 1999.

When Your Best is Not Good Enough
Grand Rapids, Mich.: Revell, 1997.

Women Who Try Too Hard
Grand Rapids, Mich.: Revell, 1998.

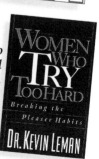

VIDEO TAPE RESOURCES

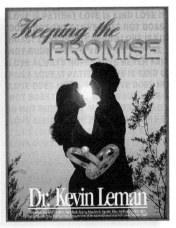

Keeping the Promise
Eight part video curriculum for couples (Dallas Christian Video).

Bringing Up Kids Without Tearing Them Down
Eight part video series on parenting (Dallas Christian Video).

1. *The Seeds of Self-Esteem*
2. *The Three Basic Types of Parents*
3. *How to Be in Healthy Authority over Your Child*
4. *Why Kids Misbehave (and what you can do about it)*
5. *How to Make Your Child Feel Special*
6. *The Powerful Secrets of Reality Discipline*
7. *Living in a Stepfamily (without getting stepped on)*
8. *Keeping Your Family Together When the World Is Falling Apart*

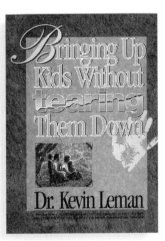

*Raising Successful & Confident Kids, Why Kids
Misbehave, Living in a Stepfamily, How to Get Kids to
Do What You Want Them to Do*

Don't forget to look for the suggestions of additional resources at the end of each session. Well, that's it. Let's get started down the path to *Becoming A Couple of Promise*.

Introduction

Most people marry exactly the wrong person. Isn't that reassuring news for those of us who are already involved in a marriage relationship? Statistics tell us that the average marriage lasts only seven years and produces 1.9 children. As a practicing psychologist of many years, I've discovered that it's because most of us marry exactly the wrong person.

Yet very few of us enter into marriage saying, "Have your attorney call my attorney." Even though it's become fashionable to draw up prenuptial agreements, most people still get married believing they're starting a long and loving relationship.

Let me reassure you that marriage, as God designed it, can be the fulfilling relationship you expected. As a husband of more than thirty-two years, I can attest to this. As a psychologist who has counseled thousands of couples, I've been regularly encouraged upon seeing two people, who from all indications were "wrong for each other," learn to reconcile their differences and become one in marriage.

Proverbs 13:12 tells us, "Hope deferred makes the heart sick." There is little in life more painful than the crushing disappointment of a failed relationship. I want to reassure you that when marriage becomes the relationship God intended it to be, it will be a great source of joy for both parties.

Beautiful cathedrals are built one brick at a time. So, too, are the walls that divide us. My intention with this book is to help you discover how to live life and conduct your marriage with purpose. In the following eight sessions you'll find tools to help you build your marriage into a beautiful cathedral. You'll also look at how to dismantle some of those walls you may have erected because of your unique circumstances and problems.

How to Use This Book

If you're currently discouraged over the state of your marriage, this course will help you discover some key ways to improve it. If you're still single and want to prepare yourself for what's ahead, this study will help lay the groundwork. If you think you've already got a good marriage but want to strengthen it, you'll find plenty of help here too. Whatever your situation, you can use this study in numerous settings:

- **As a couple or couples.** If at all possible, work through the book with your spouse, because you'll be exploring the distinct roles that each of you contributes to your marriage. Take turns "leading" alternating sessions or sections within each session. This shouldn't require any advance preparation because the exercises are fairly self-explanatory. Proceed at your own pace. However, if there is opportunity, consider joining with another couple to go through the course. You may benefit greatly by sharing your experiences and insights without losing the intimacy of a small setting. In fact, why not check around for a few other couples who might enjoy studying this with you?
- **With a group.** Designate a facilitator (better yet, a couple or a threesome who can share preparation and presentation). The facilitator doesn't have to be an "expert." (I'm still learning; why not you?) It's okay to have questions, share your own marriage and family challenges, and be part of the learning process. After all, that's what the body of Christ is all about: encouraging one another to "grow up in Him."
- **By yourself.** Even if you find your spouse isn't interested or doesn't have the time, tackle the course alone. Whenever we need changes in a relationship, especially in marriage, those changes always must begin in ourselves. By yourself, it's possible to get 88.6 percent (well, more or less) of the value of this course that you would get if you studied with others.

In each section of this book you'll find clearly outlined principles to help you better understand both marriage in general and your spouse in particular. You'll study the underlying biblical material that supports these principles, and you'll get involved in numerous practical exercises to help you grasp and apply the concepts. Each session conforms roughly to the following format:

1. I'll introduce a new facet of becoming a Couple of Promise.
2. We'll dig into the Bible to get a solid foundation from God's Word.
3. I'll give you some practical input from the "Dr. Kevin Leman School of Marital Bliss" on the topic.
4. We'll examine how these principles work in typical marriage and family situations.
5. You can apply what you've learned to your own marital and family needs.

Watch for the following elements within each session that announce various activities:

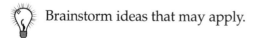 Brainstorm ideas that may apply.

Use a videotape as a supplement to this session.

Write responses or fill in answers.

Examine these ideas.

Divide the whole group into smaller groups.

Couple Chat: Couples discuss an issue or share responses.

Men's Group/Women's Group: Form separate groups for men and for women to discuss or work on an activity with their own gender.

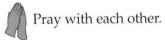 Mixed Groups: Work or discuss in small mixed-gender groups, with spouses in *different* groups.

Pray with each other.

If you're studying this course as a group, ways to present the "content" sections will be the biggest challenge. Here are a few ideas on how this might work. Try to mix and match a few of these suggestions just to keep things interesting.

1. Familiarize yourself with a content section and present it in your own words. Ask the other facilitator(s) to do the same with other sections, taking turns throughout the session. This also could be a mix of presenting some material in your own words and reading the illustrations or stories.
2. Simply read the content sections aloud, pausing along the way for questions or discussion.
3. Ask various participants to read the content section(s) aloud for the rest of the group.
4. Ask participants to read the content parts of the session ahead of time in preparation for the next session. During the actual session, ask various participants to recap what the content section is about, then move into activities or discussion.

Be sensitive to the fact that there may be one or two couples who feel uncomfortable reading aloud or being called on. That's okay. The idea is to help folks be as comfortable as they can be. If you sense some uneasiness, change your approach or feel free to shuffle people around to different groups. You also might want to partner with one of the people who feels uncomfortable.

Note: What works best for your group will depend on the size of the group (two? four? twelve? twenty-five?) and the style you and your cofacilitators feel most comfortable using.

Each participant will want to have their own copy of this study guide. Many of the activities (self-tests, choices, journaling, and so on) can be done right in this book.

In many of the sessions, you will note places where segments can be used from my video series, "Keeping the Promise", published by Dallas Christian Video. These are available from Couples of Promise, P.O. Box 35370, Tucson, Arizona 85740, or by calling 1-800-770-3830.

And don't forget to look for the suggestions of additional resources at the end of each session.

By the way, did you realize that I didn't quote the entire verse from Proverbs near the beginning of this introduction? It contains a wonderful promise: "Hope deferred makes the heart sick, but a longing fulfilled is a tree of life" (Proverbs 13:12). Marriage can give us all the life and joy we could ever hope for if it replicates God's design.

So let's get started. On the next page you'll find a test to help you determine if you're on your way to becoming a Couple of Promise.

—Dr. Kevin Leman

ARE YOU ALREADY A COUPLE OF PROMISE?

Instructions: Jot "True" or "False" next to statements 1 through 9. Then respond to the questions that follow.

___ 1. You should always put your spouse's feelings first.

___ 2. A husband and wife need to be exclusive sexual partners.

___ 3. It's important for a husband and wife to have the same spiritual beliefs.

___ 4. A husband needs to be submissive to his wife's needs.

___ 5. A wife needs to be submissive to her husband's needs.

___ 6. Men and women think and communicate in different ways.

___ 7. It's important to be completely truthful with your spouse.

___ 8. What you get out of your marriage is more important than what you put into your marriage.

___ 9. The quality of your marriage relationship has an impact on the type of spouse your children will seek.

■ What is the most important need for a married man?

■ What is the most important need for a married woman?

■ Why do most affairs occur?

■ On a scale from 1 (lousy) to 10 (great), how would you rate your marriage?

Do you think you answered the questions correctly? As you go through this course, you'll discover the best responses. But even if you think you know the right answers, in the pages ahead you'll find ways that will help you learn to apply them to your marriage.

The Original Designer Genes

Did you see the movie *Miami Rhapsody?* The closing monologue went something like this:

> Do I really want to get married at all? . . . I wonder, is it worth it? Is a lifetime of love and friendship and children worth all the compromise that goes with it? And I guess the answer's yes. I guess I still have hope. I guess I look at marriage sorta the same way I look at Miami. It's hot and it's stormy and it's occasionally a little dangerous. But if it's really so awful, then why is there still so much traffic?

As you launch into this study, bringing all the experiences of your past and your hopes for the future, let me assure you: being married is worth it! There's still a lot of traffic to those wedding altars, and rightly so. Because marriage is a wonderful, God-given institution. And it's brimming with the potential for fulfillment that's deeper than any experience you can have this side of heaven. Of course, it takes a firm commitment and lots of hard work. But what is worth having that isn't worth working for? Multitudes of people—just like you—are holding to the promises they've made at the altar and finding it thoroughly satisfying.

For the record, then, let me encourage you to keep the promise you made when you first spoke your wedding vows. I've been married for more than thirty-two years . . . in a row . . . to the same woman. I'm also the father of five children, and I've learned through experience that the best thing I can do for my kids is to be a good husband to their mom, Sande. I'm embarrassed to say, however, that it took ten years of marriage before I finally realized that the most important thing to my wife Sande was not sex.

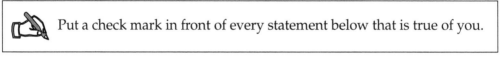 As a supplement to this session, view "The Original Designer Genes" on the videotape "Keeping the Promise," Tape 1. If you wish, launch your session by playing the opening skit on this section of the tape. Then ask your group members, "When was the last time it was obvious to you that you and your spouse are truly different?"

Recognizing Our Differences

That ultimate realization, and the many I've made before and since, has led me to a profound observation. Maybe it won't sound profound, but profound it is nonetheless: *men and women are different.*

Whoa! We're Different?

I told you it wouldn't sound profound, but if you think about it, it really is.[1] If you haven't already treated this subject to some lengthy mental pondering, take a minute for a quick "test" to find out whether you're a man or a woman.

Put a check mark in front of every statement below that is true of you.

___ 1. When the chips are down, the children usually run to *me* rather than to my spouse.

___ 2. I can never find anything in a refrigerator, but my spouse usually knows exactly where everything is.

___ 3. I tend to focus on feelings with the facts, while my spouse focuses mostly on "just the facts."

___ 4. I'm a little more personal and transparent than my spouse (also a little more ready to be honest and open in conversations).

___ 5. In social situations, I often end up talking about my job, whereas my spouse usually strays back to the subject of relationships with family and others.

___ 6. When I go shopping, I know what I want, and that's what I buy. My spouse, however, often ends up in an unrelated department, "just looking."

___ 7. On the road, I often stop and ask for directions.

___ 8. In a restaurant, I will ask for—and listen attentively to—the server's description of a long, detailed list of specials. My spouse has decided on a main course upon entering the front door.

___ 9. Around the house, I often tend to "misplace" such things as socks, belts, shoes, and other items of clothing, causing me to yell, "Honey, have you seen my _____?"

___ 10. If I am given the task of displaying Dr. Leman's books at a seminar, I stack them; my spouse would spread them out.[2]

The statements above make some broad generalizations, but this little quiz should give you a pretty good idea of your gender. If you checked numbers 1, 3, 4, 7, and 8, you're female. Congratulations! If you checked 2, 5, 6, 9, and 10, you're male—welcome to the club! If you checked a combination of the above . . . check with your doctor.

Just to clarify a couple of the statements: In number 1, haven't you noticed how the kids tend to yell for Mom, not Dad, when somebody has an "owie" or other major crisis? One study says that nearly nine out of ten working moms, 89 percent, are responsible for children when sick compared to one out of ten working fathers. That's just the way it is. It's not a conspiracy. (I've seen my daughter hit her head on a table and have gone to comfort her, only to have her give me an NFL-like move, leave me sprawled on the linoleum, and run ninety-six yards to her mother.)

As for number 6, when I take my wife shopping for a dress, I expect her to look for a dress. I'm at a loss, then, when I find her in the children's department holding up OshKosh B'gosh overalls. But most women find this perfectly logical.

And about "asking directions" in number 7. Women think they understand this tendency of us guys to avoid asking. They put it down to machismo. The truth is, we men just don't want to let all those cars we worked so hard to pass get by us again. Pure competition. It's a guy thing!

As for number 9: This one's obvious, isn't it?

So who first noticed all the gender differences we're familiar with today? Adam and Eve, of course. They became intimately acquainted with the differences between man and woman long before anyone else. Not only were their physical distinctions so apparent in the Garden of Eden that Adam practically rhapsodized over this creature he dubbed "woman" (Leman translation of Adam's words when he saw his new bride: "Holy moly, look at *that!*"). Their differences became even more pronounced when sin entered the world.

Adam and Eve suffered different and dire consequences for their transgressions. With the first sin, their perfect life was spoiled! What wasn't spoiled, however, was the relationship they enjoyed in spite of, as well as because of, their differences.

Do a brief skim-and-search exercise by quickly reading through Genesis 2:15–3:24 in your Bible. Look for biblical words, phrases, or general themes, and jot them under the appropriate columns below. Try to find clues to the differences in Adam and Eve that they either (a) had to overcome or (b) must have enjoyed—in order to keep the relationship going.

Then as a group discuss your findings and the follow-up questions below.

THE RELATIONSHIP GOES ON!

The "In Spite of" differences . . .	The "Because of" differences . . .
(Differences to overcome in the relationship)	(Differences to enjoy in the relationship)
■	■
■	■
■	■
■	■
■	■
■	■

If you had been Adam or Eve, what would have been your first words upon seeing your mate?

What factors determine whether differences in a relationship will enhance it or damage it?

How do you see some of the "Garden of Eden differences" playing out today in relationships?

In your opinion, do we place too much or too little emphasis on male-female differences? Explain.

As a spouse (or future spouse), how much do (or will) your male-female differences play a part in your conflicts? Can you give an example?

The list of differences between men and women could go on and on, of course. The "test" at the beginning of this section was just a door-opener to the differences between men and women. For example, here's another good one: If I ask my wife where to take my daughter to the dentist, she'll give me directions that include the color and kind of flowers in front of the building. What she'll probably forget to include— and it's the only thing I'm looking for—is the street address.

> A wife is a gift bestowed upon man to reconcile him to the loss of paradise.
>
> —Johann von Goethe

One of the most interesting differences I've observed is that women actually enjoy going to the restroom in groups. In social settings, not only will a woman announce that she's headed to the ladies' room, but she invites other women to go with her! It's common to see them all in line like a covey of quail. If a man goes to the restroom and finds two other men there, however, that's two too many. He'll hold it for eighteen miles until he gets home, if necessary.

But women don't even mind standing in those long bathroom lines that snake out from the doorway. It gives them a chance to communicate. "Oh, I just love your dress," you'll hear them saying. "And your hair is *adorable!*"

"Oh, don't even look at my hair! It's terrible!"

"But it's such a cute cut!"

"Well, I told her to leave it longer, and I wanted that 'autumn frost' tint. But look at it: this is more like autumn rust!"

"Well, I think it makes your face look a lot thinner."

"You do?"

"Yes, I really do, and it highlights your eyes."

"I suppose so, but what about . . ." And the conversation continues.

But when a man notices his male friend with a little less shagginess around the ears, he may grunt out something like, "Haircut, huh?"

"Yup!"

End of conversation.

Form two smaller groups, one of men and the other of women. Work together with your same-sex group members to jot two lists according to the charts that follow. The catch: your lists must flow from specific things you've personally observed in the opposite gender over the years.

When your gender group has its lists completed, come back together as one large group. Present your lists to one another, but after each item, let the opposite-gendered members tell whether they agree or disagree and briefly explain why. (Note: Go ahead, have a little fun with this!)

Top Ten List of Reasons Why Men/Women Are So Weird, Strange, and Totally Different

Reason #1:

Reason #2:

Reason #3:

Reason #4:

Reason #5:

Reason #6:

Reason #7:

Reason #8:

Reason #9:

Reason #10:

Top Ten List of Reasons Why Men/Women Are So Great, Wonderful, and Lovable (Viva La Difference!)

Reason #1:

Reason #2:

Reason #3:

Reason #4:

Reason #5:

Reason #6:

Reason #7:

Reason #8:

Reason #9:

Reason #10:

Different Creatures, Differing Perspectives

What's the solution to all of the differences between us? For one thing, we need to get behind our spouse's eyes.

You see, we *are* different, and at times the differences are glaring. Yet we can constantly attempt to see life from inside our spouse's head, looking out at the world from his or her perspective. We won't get it just right, but we can keep coming closer to their point of view. Here's a case in point. Suppose we asked marriage partners to answer this question separately from their spouses: *What is the most special physical act a husband can engage in with his wife?*

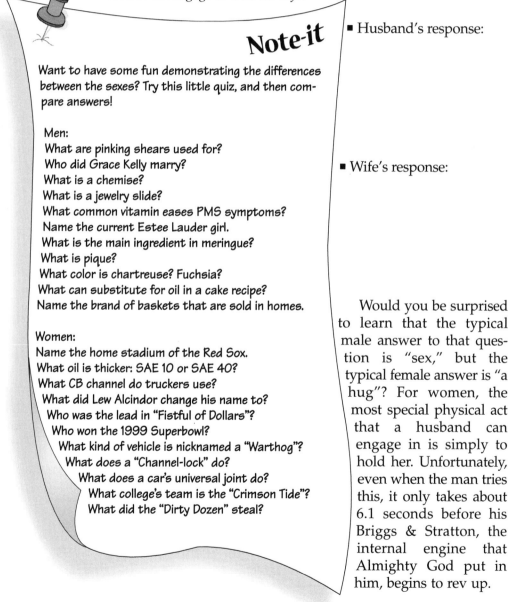

Note-it

Want to have some fun demonstrating the differences between the sexes? Try this little quiz, and then compare answers!

Men:
What are pinking shears used for?
Who did Grace Kelly marry?
What is a chemise?
What is a jewelry slide?
What common vitamin eases PMS symptoms?
Name the current Estee Lauder girl.
What is the main ingredient in meringue?
What is pique?
What color is chartreuse? Fuchsia?
What can substitute for oil in a cake recipe?
Name the brand of baskets that are sold in homes.

Women:
Name the home stadium of the Red Sox.
What oil is thicker: SAE 10 or SAE 40?
What CB channel do truckers use?
What did Lew Alcindor change his name to?
Who was the lead in "Fistful of Dollars"?
Who won the 1999 Superbowl?
What kind of vehicle is nicknamed a "Warthog"?
What does a "Channel-lock" do?
What does a car's universal joint do?
What college's team is the "Crimson Tide"?
What did the "Dirty Dozen" steal?

- Husband's response:

- Wife's response:

Would you be surprised to learn that the typical male answer to that question is "sex," but the typical female answer is "a hug"? For women, the most special physical act that a husband can engage in is simply to hold her. Unfortunately, even when the man tries this, it only takes about 6.1 seconds before his Briggs & Stratton, the internal engine that Almighty God put in him, begins to rev up.

Note-it

"Honey, would you just hold me?" Ever heard that, gentlemen?

It's a well-known fact that most women like to be held, liked to be touched, like to be cuddled. And if your wife said to you, "Buford, would you hold me?" I know you would walk over and hold her. But here's the point: she's going to tell herself, *Well, he held me—but only because I asked him to, and not because he really wanted to.* Need I say more?

I've discovered that "getting behind her eyes" means realizing that Sande wants me to be able to read her mind. She doesn't want to have to tell me things; it takes the fun out of it for her. She wants me to know in my mind that when we have company over for dinner, I'll be pouring the coffee halfway through the meal to replenish people's cups, and I'll be getting up to help clear the table later. She doesn't want to have to ask. It's a *love* thing.

I know that if I come home and the kitchen is a mess, she would love for me to clean it up. Now for me to do this really does take some thought, because I'm the youngest child of the family and I've always loved to throw things around. That's just part of the joy of life for me.

In fact, once, as an experiment, Sande threw a banana peel on the kitchen floor and thought *I'll just sit back and watch to see who does what with that peel.* She positioned herself where she could read the paper and watch what was going on as people discovered that banana peel. She said the kids stopped for a moment to take a look, and then they all walked around it.

"But you, Kevin," she said, "you kicked it to the side. I give you credit for that!"

It's the little things that add up in a marriage to make big things. Men, when your wife has left the house early in the morning because of a dental appointment and she didn't have time to clean up after breakfast, and you come home for lunch, why not put the dishes in the sink and scrub them, and put them in the dishwasher? For Sande, the important thing with her is to always wipe the counters off. She's a clean-counter woman. So I've learned to do those things—without being asked. Sande wants me to read her mind. From her perspective, my choices will be an indication of my thoughtfulness, my knowledge of what she'd like in a given situation. So she's watching to see what happens.

I know, it's terribly unfair.

But that's the way it is.

I'm convinced that our wives are asking us, every day, in lots of ways, "Do you love me? Do you *really* love me?" We are different, created by God in that way. So we need to get behind our spouse's eyes and see how they're viewing things (more about this in session 3).

In the spaces that follow, list three major areas in which you and your spouse (or future spouse) differ. Share your answers with each other.

Then, from your list, choose one difference and imagine what life would be like *if that difference didn't exist.* Discuss: "How would our marriage be strengthened or weakened without that difference?"

- Our Big Difference #1:

- Our Big Difference #2:

- Our Big Difference #3:

Dealing with Our Differences

In general, couples tend to take two basic routes when dealing with differences: (1) they let their differences drive them apart—because differences are met with attack and criticism, or (2) they learn to appreciate their differences.

The first step toward appreciation is finding out where our differences come from. There's nothing like a little knowledge to increase marital harmony. So you'll quickly recognize some important reasons for your differences by asking yourself three simple questions:

> *I chose my wife, as she did her wedding gown, for qualities that would wear well.*
>
> —Oliver Goldsmith

When Were You Born?
Birth order enters the equation of every marriage. Like a Mack truck.

In other words, two firstborns marrying are sort of . . . interesting. I always want to ask the question, "What's it like to have breakfast with a helmet on?" Firstborns are bossy, know exactly how things ought to be, are highly opinionated, want their ducks in a row, can spot a flaw at a hundred paces—and they don't like surprises!

I'm married to a firstborn. This is a typical scenario in our family. I work for five hours outside on our landscaping. Like a kid, I go running into the house hollering, "Hey, come see what I've done!" Sande goes outside, surveys the situation, and immediately points her finger toward one lonely weed. That's how firstborns are. They find the flaws. They often overdo things. Some want to iron the davenport and put newspaper under the cuckoo clock! At work you get rewarded for that, but if you sit down for dinner at home and find the flaw—you'll be wearing the broccoli.

It's these little things that get in the way of becoming a solid couple. It's easier, for example, when the marriage is between a firstborn and the baby of the family. Or even a firstborn and a middle child. Middle children are great negotiators. They know how to make peace with a firstborn. They are nice people. They're the Jack Fords, Leeza Gibbons, Michael J. Foxes, Mark McEwens, and Krissy Lemans of the world.

So you can see that your spouse's birth order can definitely set the stage for differences. Were you the firstborn? A middle child? Or the baby of the family? No matter what the branch of the family tree, birth order has a lot to do with who you are today and the kind of marriage partner and parent you will make. I delve extensively into this subject in *The New Birth Order Book*,[3] but for our immediate purposes, here's a brief sketch of birth order characteristics you should know about.

The Firstborn. In general, firstborns struggle to measure up. They tend to be perfectionists, reliable, conscientious, list-makers, well organized, critical, serious, and scholarly. Firstborns are also self-sacrificing, conservative, and supporters of law and order. They believe in authority and ritual. They are legalistic, going by the letter of the law rather than the spirit. They are also loyal and self-reliant, and many of them are goal-oriented achievers. They don't like surprises. They're planners.

The Middle Child. The middle child is harder to classify and can, in fact, be a bundle of contradictions. There's no telling which way a middle child will head, but you can be sure he or she will "bounce off" the older siblings. The bouncing off phenomenon almost guarantees that the second born will be the opposite of the first. One characteristic that bodes well for your marriage if one spouse is a middle child is that middle children are the most monogamous of all the birth orders. Because they didn't fit in all that well while growing up in their families, they have a strong desire to make their own marriage work. Competitive, and the most natural negotiator of the birth order zoo, they find solace in others mostly outside of their immediate family.

The Lastborn. The baby of a family often turns out to be the clown or the entertainer who keeps everybody in stitches. While middle children often feel they're being rejected, lastborns feel they aren't taken seriously. After all, they are the youngest, the smallest, the weakest, and the least equipped to cope. They are always being told, "You're not quite big enough or old enough to do that yet." Somewhere along the line the little caboose starts to think, *I'll show them!* And they do it by grabbing attention any way they can. Lastborns are very often outgoing and wind up in jobs like selling cars and other vocations that are highly people-oriented.[4]

Note-it

Are you a firstborn—and married to a firstborn? Ouch! Here are some tips for reducing tension and increasing harmony:

1. Steer away from "improving" on things your spouse does or says. Since you're probably a perfectionist, doing so may be difficult, but bite your tongue and do it anyway. Practice tongue control whenever possible.

2. Stop "shoulding" your mate. Criticism is second nature to you (your main target is yourself). Put away your high-jump bar. Quit trying to jump higher, and quit asking your mate to do so as well.

3. To avoid control issues, have good role definitions. Develop a specific division of labor as to who does what in the family.

4. Realize there are more ways to skin a cat than your way. Work on valuing your spouse's ideas and learn that a suggestion that isn't your own can still be a good one—even the best one.[5]

In the space below, diagram your family tree, including all members of the family you grew up in. After you're finished, take a few moments to examine the chart for hints of how family influences may still affect you today.

FATHER

MOTHER

FATHER

FATHER

MOTHER

FATHER

BROTHERS / SISTERS

FATHER

MOTHER

MOTHER

NAME

BROTHERS / SISTERS

MOTHER

BROTHERS / SISTERS

FATHER

MOTHER

FATHER

MOTHER

FATHER

MOTHER

FATHER

MOTHER

After you've had a chance to think about your early family influences in the preceding exercise, talk with your spouse for a few minutes. Together, think through some of the apparent effects of birth order on your relationship. Use one or more of the following questions to spark your discussion.

1. What is your birth order? Your spouse's?

2. Based upon your understanding of birth order, what kinds of conflicts can you and your spouse expect to encounter?

3. How can your particular combination of birth orders foster compatibility?

4. If you're both firstborn and get along famously, would you admit it's because one of you is laid back while the other has a more domineering nature? Talk about that.

5. What specific lessons in life did you learn from growing up in your family? From watching Mom and Dad interact?

How Were You Parented?

Birth order isn't the only profound influencer of differences in a marriage relationship. It also matters greatly how your parents related to one another. If husbands and wives want to trace some important parental influences, they need to look at four family relationships:

- how Dad treated Mom
- how Mom treated Dad
- how Dad treated the daughter
- how Mom treated the son

When Dad treated Mom badly, for example, the repercussions can pop up years later after the children are grown. Just being aware of how you were parented (including all the dynamics of the relationship between you and your parents) can be a tremendous advantage. People have said for years that a man marries his mother and a daughter marries her dad. Well, it's not quite that simple. But believe me, how your mom and dad treated each other—and treated you—has everything to do with who you are and who you marry.

Note-it

How do you deal with differences? Differences in background, differences in perceptions, differences in values—all these can add up to a lot of pressure and stress unless you know how to cope. Here are two basic suggestions:

1. Care enough to confront each other (lovingly, of course).

2. Care enough to work at changing yourself for the good of your partner and your marriage.[6]

You and your spouse can use just one book or write responses in each other's book. In a sentence or two describe how your dad treated your mom and your mom treated your dad. Then have your spouse do the same. Discuss how your responses compare and contrast.

- How my DAD treated my MOM:

His response:

Her response:

■ How my MOM treated my DAD:

His response:

Her response:

Discuss with your spouse:

■ With your family background in mind, do you believe you imitate your parents in the way you treat your spouse? Offer an example for discussion.

■ Considering how your parents related to each other in marriage, do you want to have a similar relationship with your spouse? Why? Why not?

What's Your "Style of Life"?

Psychologist Alfred Adler believed that very early in life each of us develops a style of life or "lifestyle." In other words, we all decide what works best for us as we try to reach our goals. There are many different lifestyles. In fact, it would be fair to say that each person has worked out his or her own unique lifestyle. But our individual uniquenesses aside, most of us fit into certain broad lifestyle categories. The key for a happy marriage is to determine your mate's style! Let's look at four of the most common lifestyles and focus on their "downsides."

Controllers have to be in charge. Why must they be in charge? It stems from one of two reasons: (1) they're on a power trip or (2) they're afraid that if they don't remain in charge, someone else will control *them.* Controllers tend to be perfectionists and short-tempered. They have a need to be right, and they often keep others at arm's length.

Pleasers have to be liked by everyone. These folks are extremely sensitive to criticism and work hard to keep everyone around them happy, no matter what. They seldom show their true feelings, because they don't want to offend or be rejected. They hide their feelings behind a mask of phony smiles, all the while hating themselves for not having the courage to tell people what they really think. It's no surprise, then, that pleasers usually have low self-esteem. They don't believe they're worth much, and they constantly try to build themselves up by doing all they can to please everyone else. They want the oceans of life to be smooth!

Attention-getters have to be noticed. These are the carrot-seekers of life. They look for reward and praise. Because I'm the baby of my family, I confess to being an incurable attention-getter. I love my vocation, which centers on helping people through counseling. But I love my avocation even more: making people laugh. Interestingly enough, attention-getters could be called first cousins to controllers. Attention-getting can be a primary cause of extramarital affairs. If this partner doesn't get enough attention at home, he or she may wander off to find it elsewhere.

Martyrs have to lose. Sadly, these people think they never deserve to win. They have a poor self-image, so they're good at finding people who will walk all over them. Martyrs seem to gravitate to losers with an uncanny accuracy. They may marry alcoholics, abusers, or drug addicts.[7]

From the scenarios that follow, choose one that most closely resembles a relational or marital situation you've experienced in the past. Jot the likely responses of spouses who have one of the four different lifestyles. Then think about how you would have responded in the circumstances (you can take on the role of either gender).

Be as specific as you can in jotting what would be done first in each case. When you're through, ask yourself which—if any—of the lifestyle characteristics you have that cause (or *could* cause) difficulties in a marriage.

Newlywed Linda is planning her first vacation with her husband, George. Because they'll be staying in a historic city, Linda is excited about all the things she'll see and learn. To make sure she misses none of it, she's planned out each day's activities, including time limits, in order to get everything in.

Just as Linda puts the finishing touches on the schedule, George walks in, smiles brightly, and says: "This is going to be great! A whole week of doing nothing. Sleeping in, laying around. Now that's what I call a vacation!"

Linda looks up, opens her mouth, and begins to . . .

■ A Controller's likely response:

■ A Pleaser's likely response:

■ An Attention-getter's likely response:

■ A Martyr's likely response:

■ My own likely response:

David received a hefty raise two months ago, but he is still concerned about the family budget. He's spent many evenings working with his computer budgeting program, going over all the spending of the previous year, making charts and projections of the year ahead. Finally, he walks into the family room where Juanita is putting away some groceries and announces: "From now on, this wonderful family of four is going to be living on $633.49 per week—including all taxes, insurance, and savings for the year. Isn't that great? . . . Hey, you bought *lobster?*"

Juanita had just been thinking: *Sure is great to go to the store these days without having to be afraid of overspending; I'm so tired of scrimping!*

She turns to David and . . .

- A Controller's likely response:

- A Pleaser's likely response:

- An Attention-getter's likely response:

- A Martyr's likely response:

- My own likely response:

Sherri and Ted arrive at the party late. As they walk into the living room, they find a group of women sitting in a circle talking. Ted quietly takes a seat, wondering where the men have gone. But Sherri, once she hugs and greets most of the ladies, suddenly announces: "Hey, everybody! I haven't said anything to Ted about this, but I can't think of a better time for good news than when all my girlfriends are gathered around.

"So, here goes. . . . I'm *pregnant!*"

Ted turns quickly, and . . .

- A Controller's likely response:

- A Pleaser's likely response:

- An Attention-getter's likely response:

- A Martyr's likely response:

- My own likely response:

I think it's so interesting to see how God has created all of us to be different. Isn't it fascinating that God gave us different fingerprints? In fact, He gave identical twins *different* fingerprints! Why? To help the FBI? No, God obviously delights in our differences. So if you're comparing your spouse with the person down the street, you're doing yourself, your spouse, and your marriage an injustice. Learn instead to understand, appreciate, and celebrate your differences.

Go back over the four lifestyles described on the preceding pages. First identify your own lifestyle. Then jot what you think your spouse's lifestyle is. Compare your answers, and discuss: "Do you agree with your spouse's responses?"

His:

Hers:

Let me say it again: a good marriage takes great commitment. Therefore, at the very beginning of this course, it would be a good idea to consider what kind of commitment it takes to become a Couple of Promise. Here are ten goals to aim for. . . .

THE TEN COMMITMENTS OF A COUPLE OF PROMISE
1. We commit ourselves to make love a daily choice, even when life looks easier somewhere else.
2. We commit ourselves to treasure each other as gifts from God.
3. We commit ourselves to be quick to forgive and not to hold grudges.
4. We commit ourselves to make time for each other.
5. We commit ourselves to talk daily about our thoughts and feelings.
6. We commit ourselves to show respect for each other publicly and privately, avoiding putdowns, selfish demands, and belittling words.
7. We commit ourselves to try to get behind each other's eyes, to understand the other's specific needs.
8. We commit ourselves to do all we can to make sure our marriage has a positive impact on those around us.
9. We commit ourselves to pray for each other and support each other's spiritual growth.
10. We commit ourselves to honor God and each other through our thoughts, words, and actions.

Offer sentence prayers. Designate someone to close. First talk about joys and concerns that have arisen in your family during the past week. Then pray for help to "get behind each other's eyes" in your marriages—to better understand your differences and see them as gifts to treasure.

Keeping the Promise

1. If you and your spouse are working through this book together, did you decide who should write out responses that are to be answered together? If not, decide this now. What criteria did you choose to make this decision?

2. Think of areas of marriage in which you and your spouse have struggled in portioning out roles, such as who will balance the checkbook, pay the bills, do the grocery shopping, clean the house, and so on. Use a form like the one below to generate a list of reasons why each of these responsibilities should be given to either one. Based upon your lists, assign roles and responsibilities.

RESPONSIBILITY:

Wife's strengths/weaknesses:

Husband's strengths/weaknesses:

This responsibility is assigned to:

---

3. Think of two practical, specific ways that you can *put your spouse first* this week. Write them here:

4. Here's a "He Said/She Said" discussion starter to try. Discuss these questions over dinner one night or in your small group. Check to see if answers vary according to male/female thought processes:

   - If we're all created in the image of God, how can we be so different?
   - What does it mean to be "created in God's image"—and do our differences impact that concept in any way? Explain.

Commitment Check

The first commitment of a Couple of Promise is a resolve to keep your wedding vows. If you wrote your own vows, get them out and reread them. If you spoke traditional vows, read the pledge below to remind yourself of what you vowed:

> I, _____, take thee, _____,
> to be my wedded (wife/husband);
> to have and to hold from this day forward,
> for better, for worse,
> for richer, for poorer,
> in sickness and in health,
> to love and to cherish,
> till death do us part,
> according to God's holy ordinance;
> and thereto I pledge thee my love.

Portions of this session were adapted from:

Leman, Kevin. *Keeping Your Family Together When the World Is Falling Apart.* New York: Delacorte Press, 1992.

For further information, consider:

Leman, Kevin. *Were You Born for Each Other?* New York: Delacorte Press, 1991.

McDowell, Josh. *Building Your Self-Image.* Wheaton, Ill.: Tyndale, 1986.

NOTES

1. If you'd like a fun read with a thorough look at how different men and women are, see my newly released and expanded book *Sex Begins in the Kitchen* (Grand Rapids, Mich.: Revell, 1999).
2. Kevin Leman, *Keeping Your Family Together When the World Is Falling Apart* (New York: Delacorte Press, 1992), p. 89.
3. Kevin Leman, *The New Birth Order Book* (Grand Rapids, Mich.: Revell, 1998).
4. Leman, *The New Birth Order Book.*
5. Adapted from Leman, *Living in a Stepfamily Without Getting Stepped On* (Nashville, Tenn.: Nelson, 1994), pp. 149-150.
6. Leman, *Keeping Your Family Together . . .,* p. 115.
7. Leman, *Keeping Your Family Together . . .,* pp. 72-75.

Build It Right, Build It Strong

When Sande and I built our home several years ago, I often dropped by the site in the mornings to check on the progress. One morning at 5:30 I bumped into the builder. "What are you doing here?" I blurted out.

I was surprised to see the top guy on the scene at that hour. After all, he was the boss. He could be supervising from a distance and ordering his workers to take charge.

"This is the day we do the foundation of your home," he replied. "I've discovered that this is the day, of all days, I need to be here. If the foundation isn't right, the whole house will be off center. If it's off, it doesn't work."

As a supplement to this session, view "God's Design for Marriage" on the videotape "Keeping the Promise," Tape 1. Consider starting your session by showing the opening vignette on this section. Then ask participants, "Suppose you were a marriage counselor observing this couple's conversation. What strengths and weaknesses might you point out in the relationship?"

The Biblical Foundation of Marriage

So it is with the family. If the marriage isn't right, the whole family will be off center. But what are the building blocks of that marital foundation? What are the primary materials God uses in designing the solid groundwork of a good marriage? I'd like to suggest at least four of them for your consideration. They have to do with our sexuality, our values, our ability to love, and our goal of reaching the pinnacle of marital growth—a way of relating I call *gracefullove*.

> A successful marriage is an edifice that must be rebuilt every day.
>
> —André Maurois

Enjoying God-Given Sexuality

The first of the building blocks is sex. Yes, God has crafted us humans as sexual beings. It's a deep-down sense of identity and a longing for connection—all related to our gender. From the earliest portions of Scripture we find sex. And it's a good thing. In fact, sexuality is the essential element of our nature that brings us to marriage.

Stop right here for a moment and read through Genesis 2:20-25. As you can see, from the beginning God made men and women "suitable" for one another. Sadly, the idea that men and women are suitable for each other is a foreign thought today. My observation is that genders today are at war with each other, in a general sense. But that isn't how God intended it. He made man and woman to complement one another—to fit together perfectly, if you will. He invented marriage, and He invented sex.

To test yourself on your knowledge of what the Scriptures say about sex, take this true or false quiz. First read the selected Bible passages and then mark your responses. (Suggested answers appear at the end of this session.)

- Genesis 1:27
- Genesis 2:18-23
- Proverbs 5:18-19
- Song of Songs 4:9–5:5
- Mark 10:7-8
- 1 Corinthians 7:3
- 1 Corinthians 7:4-5
- Colossians 2:20-23
- Hebrews 13:4

____ 1. God cares about who's in bed with us.

____ 2. In summing up the Genesis model of marriage, Jesus referred to sexual intercourse.

____ 3. According to the Bible, sex is only for procreation, not for pleasure.

___ 4. Far from viewing sex as a divine concession to our human frailty, the Scriptures *urge* spouses to have sex (calling it a duty).

___ 5. From the beginning, the man wasn't a "finished product" without the woman.

___ 6. The Bible recommends long periods of sexual abstinence (fasting) in a marriage for deeper spiritual growth and maturity.

___ 7. Male and female sexuality expresses divine creativity and says something about what God is like.

___ 8. Red-hot sexual passion is celebrated in the Bible.

___ 9. A husband has complete control and discretion over his own body, and the same is true of a wife.

___ 10. The Bible prefers that we keep bodily sensations strictly regulated, as much as possible, calling us to a purely "spiritual" life instead.

Now, as a whole group, spend a few minutes talking together about your responses to the quiz. For each "True," be ready to tell the other group members which passage supports your response. For each "False," be prepared to offer your reasons for believing the statement is inconsistent with biblical teaching.

From these few biblical examples, it should be crystal clear: *Sex was God's idea.* But He designed sex *solely* for marriage, setting clear boundaries. Consider:

> *Do you not know that he who unites himself with a prostitute is one with her in body? For it is said, "The two will become one flesh."*
> (1 Corinthians 6:16)

> *But among you there must not be even a hint of sexual immorality, or of any kind of impurity, or of greed, because these are improper for God's holy people.* (Ephesians 5:3)

> *Drink water from your own cistern, running water from your own well. Should your springs overflow in the streets, your streams of water in the public squares?*
> *Let them be yours alone, never to be shared with strangers.* (Proverbs 5:15-17)

> *Stay always within the boundaries where God's love can reach and bless you.*
> (Jude 21, TLB)

Note-it

Solomon, the wisest and richest man in history, understood what it meant to enjoy marriage. Although he married eight hundred wives (can you imagine eight hundred "honeydo" lists?) and entertained three hundred concubines in a culture that accepted that lifestyle, Solomon and his favorite lover still presented the world with a vivid picture in the Song of Songs of love and human sexuality. Anonymous though she might be now, this couple showed us all how to celebrate the marriage relationship to its fullest.

As you can see, within marriage the sexual experience has God's protection. When we go outside of His laws, though, we run into problems. Therefore, in order to keep sex within those borders, we're going to need values and priorities in marriage.

Embodying Godly Values and Priorities

A Christian marriage and family life can be a wonderful witness to the ways of God. This is the second building block of the marital foundation. Right in our family we can demonstrate what God had in mind for human relationships. But we must be clear about exactly what we're aiming to convey.

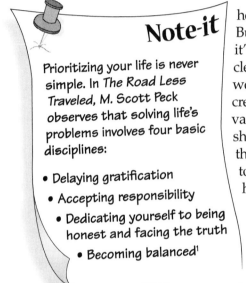

Note-it

Prioritizing your life is never simple. In *The Road Less Traveled*, M. Scott Peck observes that solving life's problems involves four basic disciplines:

• Delaying gratification

• Accepting responsibility

• Dedicating yourself to being honest and facing the truth

• Becoming balanced[1]

If you go to business seminars, you usually hear all about goals and targets and objectives. But do families have goals today? If not, maybe it's because we have so little time to develop a clear sense of direction. Sixty percent of married women work outside the home, a situation that creates instant stress for your family and robs it of valuable time. Seven- and eight-year-olds now show up regularly in shrinks' offices because they're already stressed out. So we need to learn to ask ourselves the kinds of questions that will help us sort out our priorities. These are the hard questions like: What are our family's goals? Do we really have time for *this* activity or *that* commitment? And if we're going to make time for the things that matter the most to us, what things are we going to boot out?

Tough questions! And maybe they're so hard because they center on the values you're choosing for your home. If you're going to make it in marriage today, you've got to have a marriage that's full of priorities, all based on your most prized values.

Do you proclaim Christlike values—and live by them? Every family is unique, but the Scriptures on the following page describe some of the virtues that you and your spouse might want to make priorities in your home. Skim through these passages and talk about them together for a few moments. Then identify the values that come through.

SCRIPTURE	VALUE(S)
Deuteronomy 31:6	■
Ruth 1:16-17	■
Psalm 15	■
Psalm 133:1	■
Jonah 3	■
John 13:35	■
2 Corinthians 2:9	■
2 Corinthians 8:6-7	■
2 Thessalonians 3:6-13	■
Hebrews 11:1-2	■
James 1:2-5	■
2 Peter 1:5-9	■

■ The values above are only a sampling. Use this space to jot other values that you may want to make a priority in your marriage and family:

Values

■

■

■

Scripture basis

■

■

■

- Now go back and work on citing biblical references for the values you listed above. (After all, if they don't shine through in the Bible, are they truly worthy of high priority?) A concordance or topical Bible may help you find relevant verses or passages.

Values
-
-
-

Scripture basis
-
-
-

As you continue working with your spouse to identify and form your family values in the days ahead, consider using a grid like the one below. For now, choose one or more items and begin working on a decision.

THE ISSUE	VALUES THAT WILL INFORM OUR DECISION	OUR LIKELY DECISION
Something our family is considering spending money on		
Something we're thinking about taking on as a new commitment		
Something about which we're having to say "yes" or "no" to our kids		
Something the church, our relatives, community, or employer wants us to do		
Something that might require us to be less liked or less popular		

Exchanging God's Gift of Love

What would you choose as *the most important value* to your family? My guess is that most of us would name love as the primary value without having to give it a second thought. And that brings us to the third building block of the marriage foundation: the ability to give and receive love. You're no doubt aware, though, that love as a spiritual concept has been bandied about by the world for a long time. By now, it's been perverted into something even God might find unrecognizable.

> To understand what true love is, go back to the biblical definition found in 1 Corinthians 13. Take a moment to read through that chapter, focusing particularly on verses 4 through 8. Then complete the sentences below. (Optional: When you're finished jotting your ideas, exchange books with your spouse and talk about your responses.)

1. The phrase that strikes me as the most overlooked aspect of love in our marriage is . . .

2. The facet of love that I personally have the most difficulty displaying consistently is . . .

3. One way I could begin to show more love in my daily interactions with my spouse is . . .

4. One way I'd like my spouse to express more love to me is . . .

The world typically views love as a kind of healing potion, a way to get our own needs met ("Hey, I love you; you're the best thing that ever happened to me"). But scriptural love is all about its object: the other person. It's something that builds up the other, whether spouse or child, helping him or her grow into spiritual maturity.

I like to talk to high school students about this, but I do it in a bit of a sneaky way. You see, they're so cool. I go into an assembly where the kids slouch in their chairs, their bodies sort of touching the seats in a couple of places. They're really working hard at looking cool. All they know is that some old guy is coming to talk to them.

One of the things we've failed to communicate to such young people is that marriage is actually a lot different from what we've made it out to be. So I ask the teens to picture themselves ten years older, married, and in bed with their mate. What do you suppose a thousand kids in public high school do in response to that question? They go, "All right, all right!"

Then I bring it to an abrupt, complete halt, when I say, " . . . and you're sleeping."

Once the groans quiet down, I continue. "Gentlemen, your bride wakes you up in the middle of the night. You reach for the phone. Then you realize it's your wife.

"'Honey, I'm sick,' she says. While you're helping your wife to the john, she throws a five-footer on the floor."

Then I say, "Guess who's gonna clean that up."

The point I'm making—and my primary message to couples—is simple: give and receive love by *always putting your spouse's feelings first.*

That's true love. It starts there, and it's the strongest foundation you can build your home and family life on. You can't make children the centerpiece of your home; rather, you will deeply affect them by the loving interaction that flows between you and your spouse. And the best part is that we don't have to go it alone as we keep trying to exchange God's love with our spouses. As 1 John 4:16 says, "We know and rely on the love God has for us."

Note-it

When I say, "Don't make children the centerpiece of your home," some couples react pretty strongly. They immediately ask, "Well, why not?"

Here's my answer: You don't do it because it gives them the idea that they are the centerpiece of the universe. And if that's true, then where is Almighty God? And where are other people? Doesn't this breed the kind of permissiveness and selfishness that we see in so many homes today?

Experiencing Gracefullove

Are you ready for the fourth building block of the marital foundation? It's actually the culmination of certain stages through which a marriage may progress. I say "may" because all married people experience the first two stages to one degree or another. But stages three through five are only *potential* pitfalls along the way; they may or may not trip us up. Only the sixth stage is a desired goal. Let's look at them all a little more closely:

STAGE 1—Great Expectations. Wouldn't you like to eavesdrop on two sixteen-year-olds making out in a car, talking about what it's going to be like when they're married? Talk about oblivious! Once when Sande was sick, as I helped her get dressed, I told my daughter, "Take notes. This is closer to what married life is like than anything you've probably imagined so far."

STAGE 2—Reality Hits. The period of time it takes to move from the first stage to this one varies among couples. For some people, reality hits while they're still on their honeymoon. For others it's a gradual recognition over the years that "this is probably as good as it's going to get" or "I guess he's not going to change, after all." Most everyone can relate to a sudden dose of reality that hits soon after the bliss of all the candlelight romance of courtship. What was it for you?

STAGE 3—Possible Disillusionment. This is the danger zone. This is where Satan makes his move. Proverbs 13:12 tells us, "Hope deferred makes the heart sick." This truth relates perfectly to this stage in a marriage, because most couples do come to a point of facing the fact that so many of their hopes have not come to pass. They're disillusioned about the difference between "what I thought marriage was going to be" and "what it turned out to be." And that hope deferred creates a bitter loneliness in the spouse that is noticed by only a few. In other words, it may not be glaringly obvious to others. But there's an unhappy person in the marriage, nevertheless.

In this stage the man realizes his wife probably isn't going to pursue him the way he'd like. The woman realizes her husband isn't the romantic hero she once imagined. If you listen to most people in my profession they'll tell you, "You're worthy. You deserve to have your expectations met." So you lie awake telling yourself lies at this point, including, "I've got to be me." Disillusionment also tells you, "Surely *someone* out there is going to love me the way I want to be loved." It's at this stage that people go through those notorious mid-life crises.

STAGE 4—Potential for License. For many, license flows out of disillusionment. This is the stage where people finally decide "I've got to be me" and act on it. Some of you, of course, feel as though you were sold damaged goods. And some of you are, indeed, paying for your mate's background, upbringing, past disappointments, and failures. That's because of a simple principle that many of us never discover until after we say our vows: *You date the adult; you marry the child.*

Yes, you marry the child your spouse once was. If I were to put my little girl on a ladder, moving her higher and higher up the rungs to a height of twenty feet, she'd jump to me. I would catch her, too. She knows that and jumps to me. In some cases, though, when a little child has done a swan dive, the other person has pulled back. So the child shuts down from that point on, not wanting to risk trusting others again. You, as the spouse, are then forced to live with the consequences of that early crisis.

STAGE 5—EITHER: Prospect of Separation/Divorce. From license may come the formal dissolution of a marriage—unless you as a couple discover *gracefullove.*

STAGE 6—OR: Gracefullove. "Gracefullove" is a word I invented to describe the goal of marital relationships. Instead of divorce, you can come to a point where you accept your spouse unconditionally and experience grace that's full of giving and receiving love. Why is it so crucial to reach this point? For one thing, the average marriage in the United States lasts a whopping seven years. My best prediction for a couple who tells me, "We're so in love," is they'll be divorced in seven years and have 1.9 children. It's sad and scary, and all too possible. Yet gracefullove is possible, too.

Think about the ways you have experienced the stages of marriage so far. Have you moved through them without much damage? Been hindered greatly? Stopped cold in your tracks? Now consider the questions below. First think about how you would answer. Then jot responses that you think your spouse would offer. (Plan to make time for checking your perceptions later.)

1. Given the six stages of marriage, at what stage of marriage are you? How do you know? (Remember that you and your spouse can be in different stages.)

   - I would say:

   - My spouse would say:

2. What is your most memorable "great expectation"? Your most bitter taste of reality or experience of disillusionment?

   - I would say:

   - My spouse would say:

3. What do you think it might take—as a first step—to move you and your spouse closer to gracefullove?

   - I would say:

   - My spouse would say:

The Ways of Gracefullove

The concept of gracefullove is so important that we need to explore it in depth and apply it to our marriage in the most practical ways. Let's start with a basic recognition: *God is love, and He is what's going to make your marriage different.* In other words, if you don't have God as part of your union, you have a real challenge ahead of you. But with God, gracefullove is attainable. Here's how it comes through in 1 John 4:7-12:

> *Dear friends, let us love one another, for love comes from God. Everyone who loves has been born of God and knows God. Whoever does not love does not know God, because God is love. This is how God showed his love among us: He sent his one and only Son into the world that we might live through him. This is love: not that we loved God, but that he loved us and sent his Son as an atoning sacrifice for our sins. Dear friends, since God so loved us, we also ought to love one another. No one has ever seen God; but if we love one another, God lives in us and his love is made complete in us.*

Meditate for a moment on the Scripture passage above. Ask God for insight as you consider the questions below.

---

1. According to this passage in 1 John, where does love come from?

2. When we decide to love someone, the Bible promises that His love will be made perfect in us. What, therefore, can you expect to happen if you make a conscious decision to act in loving ways toward your spouse?

We can do a lot of specific things to keep the love flowing in our marriages. But how, in general, can we keep applying gracefullove in the midst of everything that happens within a marriage, day by day? Here are four ways to keep in mind—and to keep acting on your determination to build your marriage on a solid biblical foundation.

Keep Accepting Your Differences

Can you do it? I know that Sande and I have learned to accept our differences on many levels. For example, she's a sleeper. My rulebook says, "You ought to be up by now." But if I go in and say, "Hey, get up!" it's going to be a long day. (It's going to be a long winter, if you know what I mean.) So I've learned the best way to wake Sande Leman up in the morning. I bring her coffee, two creams—not one—and I scratch her back. S-shape. And, very important, *on top* of the nightie only. After I scratch her back this way, I scratch it backhanded, just with my fingernails. Then she loves it when I scratch her arms. And she purrs like a little kitten when I scratch her hands, on top and then on the palms. Then I take lotion or cream (usually from the free little bottles I bring home from hotels) and rub her hands with it.

She wakes up like a purring kitten.

Does your wife or husband have some "different" ways of needing to be treated, too? Ways you never needed for yourself? Even *weird* ways? But then, what are your own unique needs and desires? We can look at marriages and all the differences and say, "Yeah, God sure has a sense of humor". . . and then go our merry way. We may never reach out to spot those differences and meet those special needs until we get to the stage of gracefullove. There's no question that husbands and wives are different. The challenge is to put those differences together to become a team.

When working out differences the goal is not for either side to win but for the marriage to win. If someone is winning in marriage, then both parties lose. Take a few moments to think about how it would look for *your marriage* to win in a win-lose situation that you and your spouse have experienced.

One of you recall a "win" and the other a "loss" scenario from your past. If you wish, jot some notes about those events in the spaces below. Then talk together about how those stories could have turned out differently. Write that imaginary, happy ending!

(Optional: If there's time, consider any impending conflicts on the horizon in your marriage. How will you pull your differences together to work as a team in that situation? What forms of "accepting our differences" could make it a win-win for you both?)

- PAST SITUATION: "In this case, I won and my spouse lost."
  (Describe the circumstances and outcome):

- PAST SITUATION: "In this case, my spouse won and I lost"
  (Describe the circumstances and outcome):

- REWRITE SITUATION: "Our marriage won."
  (Choose one of the situations above and imagine that you could go back and rewrite the ending of the story. How might it have looked, had the marriage won? Discuss: What forms of "accepting our differences" would it have taken to write the happy ending above? Be specific!)

Keep Exchanging Those Rulebooks

Unfortunately, most people don't fall in love. They fall in need.

And we enter into marriage with our personal rulebooks laying out how life should meet those needs: our unique set of expectations. What happens, then, when somebody does something that's not in our rulebook? One example from Randy Carlson, my former cohost on the radio call-in show "Parent Talk," lends some insight here. He knows that his wife's father loves to garden. Randy hates gardening. So that was an expectation his wife had to deal with: she'd expected that Randy and her dad would spend lots of time together, hoes in hand, flitting among the strawberry plants and watermelon vines.

But it was not to be.

When somebody does something outside of our rulebooks we might play a game I call "I'm the Umpire." "Hey, wait a minute, that's a foul!" we yell. We blow the whistle, trying to get the "player" (our spouse) to play by the (our) rules. "One more of those and you're out of the ball game!" we threaten. If we're unable to stick it to the player, we may just walk away from the game.

Other couples play "Take That, You Rat!" They collect all the emotional steer manure from their accumulated years together and store it in their dump trucks.

Then they wait. And they wait. And wait.

Until eventually, at the right moment, when it will cause just the right amount of pain, they back up to their mates and dump it all on them. Then they come in and tell me, "We just don't feel the same about each other anymore." No wonder! They've got eight cubic yards of steer manure covering the relationship.

What's the solution? Exchange those rulebooks! If you're willing to exchange your rulebooks and keep adjusting your expectations, your marriage can grow into blissful harmony (okay, almost). But perhaps the issue is: *Do I really believe that God's grace is sufficient to do it?* If that's the case, then recall the story in the Bible of Jesus telling the weary disciples, who had caught nothing after a full night of fishing, to cast their nets on the other side of the boat. Do you remember what happened? When they followed His directions, they filled their nets. Like the disciples, most of us are guilty of making God a little bit smaller in our lives than He really is. Our nets are waiting to be filled if we fish according to His instructions.

Form two groups, one consisting of the men and the other of the women participants. Work together with your same-sex group members to fill in the rulebook that is opposite your gender (that is, women fill in the men's rulebook, and vice versa). Consider some of your most basic expectations of the opposite sex in a marital relationship. You might focus on practical issues like how men/women should handle work, money, recreation, time with spouse, household tasks, communication, romance, and so on.

(Optional: Just husband and wife could write their spouse's rulebook. Exchange . . . enjoy!)

THE RULEBOOK FOR MEN IN MARRIAGE

Be it known to all, whereas MEN should conform to certain expected patterns of behavior, based on mere common sense (according to the opposite gender), it shall be declared that . . .

When it comes to how they _____ , they shall always:

When it comes to how they _____ , they shall always:

When it comes to how they _____ , they shall always:

When it comes to how they _____ , they shall always:

Now volunteers can take turns sharing "rules" from each of the rulebooks. Discuss the most glaring differences in overall expectations between the sexes. Invite any willing couples to share specific examples of clashing expectations in their relationship. How did they handle the situation? Did they adjust their expectations?

Keep Committing—Amidst the Shockers!

We never really know when a crisis might hit our marriage and the hard times will come surging in. Even unexpected *good* news can be just as stress-producing—and as shocking—as bad news. But in the midst of all the surprises, we've got to keep committing to building one another up. We can work at strengthening the marriage even as all the circumstances attack it mercilessly.

My wife has made me breakfast three times in thirty-two years. Last Father's Day she came down the staircase like Scarlett O'Hara for just such an event. I'm thinking, *What is she doing up? After all, this woman suffers from a disease called paralysis of the eyelids.* Yet this woman, who's made me breakfast only three times in thirty-two years, understands commitment.

How do I know that? Think about what it feels like at age forty-two to learn you're pregnant. That was our little surprise. Our daughter Hannah, now twelve, was born then. But wait till you're forty-seven (and forty-nine for me) for the shocker—still another child on the way. Then listen to the doctor reciting all the things that could go wrong. Sande looked back at him and said, "Why are you telling me this?"

I've got to tell you, I was the weak one. Yes, I'm the one who writes the books, who gives everybody all the great wisdom and advice. Yet on hearing this news about baby number five, I went into a funk. I did a tilt. A friend of mine describes it as my mumbling stage. I went around for a while just mumbling, "How did this happen?"

So I go into a funk for a couple of weeks. To compound it, the older kids aren't talking either. They're not talking to us parents. They still can't believe ol' Mom and Dad are still doin' it! The only one who seemed really happy was Hannah—who was. But no one else was happy. Sande was obviously struggling with what it meant for a woman to be pregnant at age forty-seven.

We go to see the doctor again. Again he tells us about every possible malady that can afflict a pregnancy at this stage of life. And keep in mind that I have every opportunity to put my arms around my wife and tell her, "It's gonna be all right." But I don't. I'm still mumbling along, thinking this can't be happening.

I've often said through the years that God uses people to help people. While on a business trip to New York I went to see my childhood friend Moonhead and his wife Wendy. I was lamenting our situation to my friends when Wendy spoke up. "Can you think of a better family for that little girl to be born in?"

What a powerful question—like a fly swatter whacking me across the face! It was stark reality. The light bulb flashed on. It was the "Aha!" phenomenon revisited. I said to myself, *No, there isn't a better family.*

I went home from that business trip with a totally different perspective. I got home and put my arms around Sande and said, "I don't quite know what it will mean to us as a family, but it's going to be all right." We had to trust God and His values. We had to recommit to that and recommit to one another.[2]

Today if I went up to Lauren, our daughter who was born perfectly healthy, and said, "You are Daddy's little _____ _____ _____," she would fill in the words. Because she knows what I mean. I've said it often to her: She is Daddy's little gift from God.

I can think of worse shockers than expecting another beautiful child. And you've likely got your own shocking stories that stressed the seams of your marriage and tore at the fabric of your family. But how about the commitment? Did it remain strong?[3]

What do you do when life's predictability begins to crumble . . . or crash? Will your marriage hold up under the strain? Can the bonds of marital commitment grow stronger, even in the toughest of times? If so, it will take loads of commitment!

Identify your needs in relation to commitment. Imagine being in the situations listed below (or perhaps you've been there!), and mark your need accordingly. Then make some time to share your responses with your spouse during the week ahead. You might also talk about "Other" situations, too—the current "shockers" you are facing.

U = I'd need more **UNDERSTANDING** of what commitment requires in this situation.
C = I'd need more **COURAGE** to take action with what I already know about commitment.
H = I'd need more **HEALING** in my own life in order to respond with gentleness, compassion, and encouragement.
S = I'd need more **STRENGTH** to make this conscious decision: to be *open and giving* rather than *closed-up and taking*.

___ 1. When your teenage son says, "I think I'm gay."
___ 2. When you're feeling alone and tempted to reach out to someone else's spouse for affection.
___ 3. When your spouse tells you he/she would like to separate for a few weeks.
___ 4. When you receive an IRS tax-due notice that will completely wipe out your savings.
___ 5. When your mother calls and demands, "Why can't you be like your brother/sister?"
___ 6. When your father-in-law calls and says, "Sorry, but I just can't stand being around your kids."
___ 7. When you're having to work late for the third night in a row, and you know supper's waiting.
___ 8. When you haven't had sex for several weeks because your spouse "doesn't feel like it."
___ 9. When you discover that your spouse has a life-threatening disease.
___ 10. When your divorced parent introduces his/her new lover.
___ 11. When your mechanic calls and begins with "Well, first of all, the transmission kind of reminds me of hamburger meat inside. . . ."
___ 12. When your child dies in a car accident.
___ 13. When you're in the midst of addictive behavior—again . . . and again.
___ 14. When you keep seeing your spouse in the midst of addictive behavior.
___ 15. When you're verbally abused by your spouse.
___ 16. When you discover your spouse has been having an affair.
___ 17. When your spouse says, "I just quit my job."

___ Other: _____.

___ Other: _____.

___ Other: _____.

Keep Consulting Your Best Consultant

Back in the days when Dr. James Dobson and Focus on the Family were headquartered in Arcadia, California, I was on their radio broadcast a number of times. On one of those occasions, Jim invited Sande and me to lunch. I'd always thought of Jim as a mentor in many ways. I looked forward to listening to his broadcast because I so admired his straightforward advice. As I was sitting there watching this guy eat crackers drenched with raspberry jam (which Sande had brought for him) I thought, *I might as well pick the man's brain.*

I'd already told him he was so much smarter than I was because he sits behind his microphone and talks to millions of Americans, while I'm on a plane traveling all over the country doing seminars. So I asked him for one life tip—not his top ten or even top three, but one. He seemingly didn't think for a second but made this rapid-fire response: "Kevin, make sure you run everything by Sande first."

I think what I appreciated about his response is that he didn't speak in Christianese. He didn't say, "Oh, Kevin, make sure God's at the center of your life, and everything will be wonderful." But he certainly hit me right where I was—and where I needed to be. He told me to consult Sande at every opportunity.

I've found that *women, quite frankly, are closer to life than men.* That's why men, in general, should listen to their wives. As they do, the differences that threaten to drive them apart will enhance their marriage and lives.

 If it's possible to brainstorm with yourself . . . do it right now. In a few moments of silence, try to come up with a response to the following "consultation needed" question . Then make an appointment with your spouse to listen to his or her advice for you about this issue.

ATTENTION! CONSULTATION NEEDED:

"Here's a problem, concern, decision, or worry that I've been holding inside—without ever telling my spouse about it . . ."

If your group is comfortable doing so, spend some time naming specific prayer requests. Focus on ways that couples would like to develop more gracefullove in their relationship. Then ask a volunteer to pray, covering the issues and concerns raised.

Keeping the Promise

1. If you are considering a major purchase in the near future, apply the appropriate decision-making questions listed below. Together, see if these questions can help you decide whether your potential purchase is an item to add to your family budget.

MAKING MAJOR DECISIONS

When making major decisions in your family, it helps to ask yourselves questions like these:

- Do we spend our time wisely? Is this just another activity that will rob our family of precious time?
- Can we afford this? Is this the best time for us to buy, move, stop, or start something?
- Is this something we truly need to have or do, or something we merely want?
- Is this issue worthy of our taking a tough stand? It is worthy of our slugging it out? Or should we just back off and take it in stride?
- Am I trying to teach my kids something here? If so, what will they likely learn? If not, what are they probably learning anyway?
- By my example, am I living out something that really matters? By my example, am I teaching something that doesn't matter?

Answers to these kinds of questions will help you clarify values you and your family hold high.

2. Discuss the goals and priorities that you each have for your family. Develop a list of five or ten and post them on the refrigerator.

3. Make a list of some of the expectations you brought into this marriage. Show your list to your spouse. Discuss honestly which expectations have resulted in disillusionment so far. Then talk about how realistic your expectations have been.

4. On a separate sheet of paper, make a list of specific incidents that you and your spouse argue about regularly. Compare your list to your spouse's. Decide whether problems stem from basic male-female differences. When you're finished, tear up your lists while reciting to each other: "Love keeps no record of wrongs."

5. Try this "He Said/She Said" discussion starter: If we are to rely on God for gracefullove, in what practical ways can we do this?

Commitment Check

Couples of Promise commit themselves to making love a daily choice. Regardless of how long you've been married, think back to your honeymoon days. Are there things you did for your spouse then that you no longer do?

Answer key to true or false quiz from pages 40-41:
The false statements are 3 (see Proverbs 5:18-19), 6 (see 1 Corinthians 7:5), 9 (see 1 Corinthians 7:4), and 10 (see Colossians 2:20-23).

For further information, consider:

Geiman, Michelle. *It Happened After the Honeymoon.* Wheaton, Ill.: Shaw, 1994. A little book of quotes that would make great conversation starters for couples.

Minirth, Frank, et. al. *Passages of Marriage.* Nashville, Tenn.: Nelson, 1991.

NOTES
1. Adapted from Kevin Leman, *Keeping Your Family Together When the World Is Falling Apart* (Colorado Springs, Colo.: Focus on the Family, 1993), p. 74.
2. Adapted from Kevin Leman, *The New Birth Order Book* (Grand Rapids, Mich.: Revell Co., 1998).
3. Kevin Leman, *The New Birth Order Book* (Grand Rapids, Mich.: Revell, 1998).

The Submission Mission

As a frequent guest speaker, I love to go to women's luncheons. They're always elegant affairs with beautifully decorated tables and everything just so. The menu features quiche and lots of forks. Usually I'm the only man there, and all the ladies are cordial, telling me how much they're looking forward to hearing what I have to say . . . until I rise and introduce the topic: "How to Be a Submissive Woman." Then all the ladies turn and stare at the program chairwoman.

> 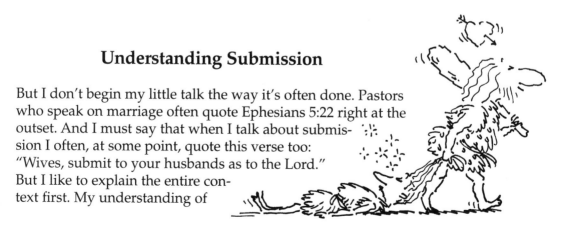 As a supplement to this session, view "The Submission Mission" on the videotape "Keeping the Promise," Tape 1. You might launch this session by playing the opening skit on this section of the tape. Then ask husbands and wives to respond separately: "What would be the most wonderful birthday present you could give your spouse?" After each response, be sure to let partners either agree or disagree!

Understanding Submission

But I don't begin my little talk the way it's often done. Pastors who speak on marriage often quote Ephesians 5:22 right at the outset. And I must say that when I talk about submission I often, at some point, quote this verse too: "Wives, submit to your husbands as to the Lord." But I like to explain the entire context first. My understanding of

Ephesians 5:21-33 is that it's slanted more toward husbands than wives, a point of view you probably won't hear very often.

Soon you'll take a closer look at the entire passage of Ephesians 5:21-33. But for just a moment, focus on verse 21 as the "umbrella statement" for what follows in the passage. After meditating on that verse for a while, how would you answer the two questions that follow? (Note: One way to "meditate" would be to try this: Have someone read the verse aloud, slowly, three times. Then, as a group, spend two minutes silently thinking about the meaning of each word in the verse.)

Who Does What?

The apostle Paul declares the overall responsibility of husbands and wives: "Submit to one another out of reverence for Christ" (Ephesians 5:21).

- To whom is this verse written?

- Describe what submission to the Lord entails.

Now read and study Ephesians 5:22-33. Choose key verses, jot the commands given, and describe the motivations suggested by Paul as to why we should carry out the commands. Work individually to fill in both columns and answer the questions that follow.

THE WIFE'S RESPONSIBILITIES	THE HUSBAND'S RESPONSIBILITIES
▪ Verse: _____	▪ Verse: _____
Command:	Command:
Motive:	Motive:
▪ Verse: _____	▪ Verse: _____
Command:	Command:
Motive:	Motive:
▪ Verse: _____	▪ Verse: _____
Command:	Command:
Motive:	Motive:

1. In your own words, describe what it means to "submit" to a husband.
   ▪ Wife's description:

   ▪ Husband's description:

2. In your own words, describe what it means to "love" a wife.
   ▪ Wife's description:

   ▪ Husband's description:

3. How would marriages be different if we took Ephesians 5:21 to heart?

4. Think: How might my marriage be different?

Now it's time to recall the command in Ephesians 5:21 and rank yourselves on the Submission Scale below. Wives, mark a "W" on your scale where you see yourself and an "H" where you see your spouse. Husbands, mark a "W" on your scale for your wife and an "H" for yourself. Then compare your rankings. Spend some time talking about similar and differing perceptions of how submission works in your relationship. Be sure to give your reasons for your rankings!

STEP UP TO THE SUBMISSION SCALE!

Wife:

1	2	3	4	5	6	7	8

I grit my teeth,
clench my fists,
and NEVER give in!

I'm a total wimp.
Whatever you want
I ALWAYS give in!

Husband:

1	2	3	4	5	6	7	8

I grit my teeth,
clench my fists,
and NEVER give in!

I'm a total wimp.
Whatever you want
I ALWAYS give in!

Obviously, submitting to one another is no easy task. But think about it: submitting to God is truly no hardship, because He always cares for us with perfect love and wisdom. Therefore, if the Bible directs wives to submit themselves to their husbands *as they would submit to Christ,* we men better be the leaders we should be.

However, my observation is that most men really don't do a very good job of leading. We tend to lead by pure proclamation. For example, suppose you're a business leader, and you win a free vacation trip. You come home and proclaim with horns blowing, "We're going to Hawaii!" This, of course, completes the male responsibility for the Hawaii trip.

While the wife plans and gets the kids ready, takes care of the mail, the dog, and the worries about all other little details—we proclaim it.

And *presto!* It's done.

Most of us are real comfortable with the Mel Gibson/Clint Eastwood approach: "Knock down the walls, we're going in!" Gallantly, we lead onward through the fog! It's the kind of tough leadership most of us men see as valuable. But the tender kind of leader is the one who knows who he's leading.

I have a friend who's an insurance agent. One day he tells me he wants to surprise his wife with a trip to San Diego. Knowing firstborns, of whom his wife is one, I say, "That's not really a good idea—the surprise part, I mean."

"Oh, no, she's going to love it," he insists.

"I'm telling you, tell her. But if you're not going to tell her, *take care of everything.*"

The day of the trip arrives. His wife asks, "What are you doing home?"

He says, "We're off to San Diego," and pulls out airline tickets.

She says, "I can't go to San Diego. What about the kids?"

"Your mother's coming."

"What about my hair? I can't go anywhere like this!" she protests.

"An hour after we land, you've got a hair appointment at the Hotel del Coronado."

She squeezes his neck, gives him a big wet kiss, and runs off yelling, "San Diego! San Diego!"

He pulled it off. He thought through what she'd be concerned about—the kids first. Next, her hair. In effect, my friend got behind his wife's eyes to see the whole trip from her perspective.

Note-it

The biblical Sarah went down in history for a lot of reasons, including birthing Isaac as an old woman. The apostle Peter commended her many years later for her submissive spirit, an attitude that spared Abraham's life on more than one occasion. The curious thing is that even when Abraham cowardly hid behind Sarah's skirts, she had the courage to be submissive to him and was rewarded for it. God always protected Sarah. In essence, her submission truly was to Him. You can read all about it in Genesis 12–20.

Get Behind One Another's Eyes

I raised this subject back in session 1, but now let's get a little more specific. What, exactly, do I mean by getting behind your spouse's eyes? Basically, it's attempting to see the world as he or she sees it. It's anticipating the unique joys and problems your spouse will likely focus on in any given event or relationship. Mutual submission entails duties by both partners in this area. Here are two practical tips on how to do it.

Husbands: Learn your wife's heart. Biblical submission begins with an intimate relationship with the person you're trying to serve. No one can submit to God unless he or she understands His heart. I've learned, furthermore, that to be a good husband, I've got to get good at learning my wife's heart. I titled one of my books *Sex Begins in the Kitchen* (recently rewritten and rereleased) because I've learned that when a man takes the garbage out without being asked, that's foreplay. Sex is an all-day affair for the woman. So men, make sure you're acting in a loving manner all the time. You begin making love to your wife *outside* the bedroom. Have you learned that yet?

I concede, however, that it's tough learning our spouse's heart—and then taking practical action on what we know. Once my wife Sande asked me for money to go grocery shopping, and I gave her the money. But she was back in twenty minutes, needing more money. I couldn't imagine why she needed more, so I asked her about it.

Note-it

Husbands, pay attention to the kinds of gifts your wife truly enjoys receiving. My son says he remembers the day his mommy was sitting on the potty crying because I gave my wife a toaster. It was a really nice toaster, a four-slicer, but I've learned some about marriage since that day. Consequently, I don't give my wife toasters anymore. She gets about as excited over a toaster as I get over a weedeater or soap on a rope for Father's Day. What did you get your wife on her last birthday? How about your last anniversary?

"Well, I stopped at Jim's gas station," she said.

I'm thinking, *So she spent twenty bucks on gas, but there would still be a lot left.* I could tell by the look on her face that something else was going on here.

Then I grinned, because I already knew the basic story line. "All right," I said. "What did you give away this time?"

Her face brightened—she knew I was going to approve—as she recounted the story. "Well, there was this woman there, and I could tell by the look of her car and her kids that she needed . . . things. . . . I bought her a battery."

She did it anonymously. She just went to Jim and said, "Take care of this lady; give me the bill." And she paid for the woman's gas and the battery. In other words, she used up about half the money I'd given her for groceries, and that's why she was back.

I'm embarrassed to tell you that my immediate internal response was a stab of anger: You did *what?* (That's where the tough part comes in—knowing and *accepting* your wife's heart.) Yet at a deeper level I could rejoice. You see, I do know my wife. She would give the car away if the situation called for it. And I'm so happy I married a woman like that who practices what we Lemans call "natural tithing"—when you see a need in someone's life, you try to meet that need. And if you can do it anonymously, all the better.

I'm ready for these moments because I know that's how Sande is. I'm learning from her, as well, to see the needs out there and to respond with unbridled generosity. My mission—and yours—is to get behind my spouse's eyes and see how she views things. It's all about being in tune with the desires of her heart.

Husbands, how well do you know your wife's heart? Find out by asking her about her favorite things. While she's jotting responses in her book, write down your own guesses in your book. Then spend time comparing what you've written. That is, listen to your wife tell you, in detail, about her favorite things—and *why* they are her favorites.

MY FAVORITE THINGS . . .

Restaurant:

Vacation place:

Movie:

TV show:

Kind of novel:

Way of working/accomplishing a task:

Way of relaxing:

Way of celebrating something special:

Way of "receiving love and feeling loved":

Kind of nightie:

Way of being approached for sex:

Wives: Find out what lights his fire. Do you know how your husband sees life? Do you know the things he would really love you to do with him?

I received one letter from a woman who decided to approach her husband rather creatively. She was scheduled to pick him up at the airport after his business trip and decided she'd really give him a thrill.

She wore a trench coat . . . and nothing else.

She parked at the airport and walked through the terminal with no problem. But she became a bit concerned as she approached the metal detectors. Nervously walking through—to her great shock and dismay—she set off the beeper. She stood there in panic, wearing nothing underneath that coat, knowing she couldn't just take it off for the friendly, smiling security man.

Note-it

Wives, if you want to understand your husband, look at his relationships with the women in his life over the years. How did he relate to his mom? His grandmother? Was he the youngest male with sisters? If he was, he was taken care of. And his expectation will be that you are going to take care of him.

How does he treat these women in his life these days? How does he talk about them? With contempt? Or respect? How did his dad treat his mom? Remember: You date the adult; you marry the child.

"Why don't you take off the belt?" the man suggested.

She gingerly slipped the belt through its loops, clutching her coat lapels tightly together, and stepped tentatively through the detector once again.

No alarm!

Her husband got a wonderful surprise on his arrival, although by now his wife had lost some of her enthusiasm for the whole idea (and has since vowed never to try that approach again). You've got to admit, though, she had a pretty good idea about what would light his fire. Because she got behind his eyes.

Wives, do you know what lights his fire? That's just another way of saying that you're attempting to get behind his eyes in terms of knowing what encourages, inspires, enthuses, and arouses his passions. Take the little test that follows. Then let your husband grade it. Listen closely to your husband's comments about the things that make life and marriage good for him. (Remember, injecting a little humor can help the communication process flow more smoothly!)

WHAT LIGHTS HIS FIRE?

1. When it comes to food and eating, it's . . .
    A. Carrots, celery, bean sprouts, and tofu . . . Yummy!
    B. *Chez Vincente* for fine French dining—the more forks, the better.
    C. Just meat and potatoes. What else is there?
    D. Bring on those chocolate-chip pancakes! Extra sausage, please!
    E. Other (explain):

2. When it comes to entertainment, hobbies, and recreation, it's . . .
    A. Doing fun things alone.
    B. Gathering with a bunch of guy friends.
    C. Sharing all "fun times" and hobbies with wife and family.
    D. Having the occasional "night out" for myself.
    E. Other (explain):

3. When it comes to spending money, it's . . .
    A. "Honey, have you seen the coupon for the cat litter?"
    B. "A penny saved is a penny earned."
    C. "Let the good times roll, Baby!"
    D. "Hey, I work hard; I deserve it. It's just debt, you know."
    E. Other (explain):

continued

4. When it comes to job and career fulfillment, it's . . .
   A. "Ahhhh . . . Nothing better than sore muscles and dusty clothes at the end of the day. And just look at what I made—with my own hands!"
   B. "I can't believe they're actually paying me for this—just to think up new ideas. I love it!"
   C. "Oh no! It's not time to head to the office again, is it?"
   D. "See you two weeks from Tuesday, Honey. I've got about twenty minutes blocked out in my day planner for some quality time with you and the kids. Remember: if I'm not a VP by age twenty-six, I'm a real failure."
   E. Other (explain):

5. When it comes to spiritual growth, it's . . .
   A. Marveling over a beautiful sunset (mountain range, seaside storm, . . .).
   B. "Save the blue-bellied swamp mouse! It's what God would want us to do!"
   C. Sitting quietly, just to "let God love me."
   D. Being there at church: every time, same pew, singing with gusto.
   E. Other (explain):

6. When it comes to romance and affection (but not sex), it's . . .
   A. Spending an hour or two at the local hardware store.
   B. Being showered with hugs and kisses for being "My hero!"
   C. Receiving a great back rub.
   D. A black-tie night out—dinner and the opera would be great.
   E. Other (explain):

7. When it comes to the sex, it's . . .
   A. 10 P.M., sex; 10:05, lights out.
   B. "Well, I guess it's that time of year again, Honey."
   C. "How 'bout you making the first move once in a while?"
   D. "Let's block out three hours tonight. . . ."
   E. Other (explain):

> The difficulty with marriage is that we fall in love with a personality, but must live with a character.
>
> —Peter DeVries

Putting Submission into Practice

Maybe at this point you're thinking: *I know my spouse. And I want to please my spouse. But with his personality, it's so tough!* Maybe you married a pleaser, a controller, or

> *Marriage is that relation between man and woman in which the independence is equal, the dependence mutual, and the obligation reciprocal.*
>
> —Louis K. Anspacher

a martyr. Our lifestyles influence the way we think about submission, sometimes causing us to form misguided notions. I counsel very few women, by the way, who come into my office and tell me, "I love to be controlled. I love it when my husband controls me."

So while we're talking about submission, we've got to consider when it's especially *hard* to submit. One case is when you're living with a perfectionist. The two most difficult people to deal with are the perfectionist and the defeated perfectionist.

PERFECTION OR EXCELLENCE?	
Perfectionists	**Pursuers of Excellence**
Reach for impossible goals	Enjoy meeting high standards within reach
Value themselves by what they do	Value themselves by who they are
Get depressed and give up	May experience disappointment but keep trying
Are devastated by failure	Learn from failure
Remember mistakes and learn from them	Correct mistakes and learn from them
Can only live with being number one	Are happy being number two if they know they tried their hardest
Hate criticism	Welcome criticism
Have to win to keep high self-esteem	Can finish second and still have a good self-image

Take this test to determine how much of a perfectionist you are.[1] Check all that apply. Then see how you rate by referring to the answer key at the end of this session.

Perfectionists Everyone?

___ 1. When you see a crooked picture on someone else's wall, you itch to straighten it.

___ 2. Someone has told you, point blank, that you're too demanding.

___ 3. You feel driven to correct someone else's mistake, even though it was harmless.

___ 4. You would rather not do a task at all than not do it right.

___ 5. You constantly have to control the urge to re-do your children's chores.

___ 6. When you make a mistake, even a small one, it nags at you all day.

___ 7. You often give in to the urge to tell others what they should be doing.

___ 8. If someone termed your work "good enough," that would bother you.

___ 9. You still feel disappointment when you remember losing an important game, contract, position, and so on, in the past.

___ 10. You would rather be in charge of a meeting than just be a participant.

As you can probably tell, perfectionism, at heart, is a self-esteem problem. Yet those who know Almighty God shouldn't struggle with self-esteem. The truth is that as a child of God you are greatly loved and very precious to Him.

Scripture overflows with images conveying the esteem with which God holds His creation and His creatures. That includes you! As a small child once put it: "God don't make no junk." Below you'll find only a sampling of the verses that affirm you as special and beloved to God. In effect, this is you—from behind God's eyes.

Work with a partner or small group to develop a list of all the adjectives, privileges, and honors that God ascribes to you in these verses. Then share your list with the whole group before discussing the head/heart question that follows.

God created man in his own image, in the image of God he created him; male and female he created them. (Genesis 1:27)

You made [humankind] a little lower than the heavenly beings and crowned him with glory and honor. You made him ruler over the works of your hands; you put everything under his feet: all flocks and herds, and the beasts of the field, the birds of the air, and the fish of the sea, all that swim the paths of the seas. (Psalm 8:5-8)

You created my inmost being; you knit me together in my mother's womb. I praise you because I am fearfully and wonderfully made. (Psalm 139:13-14)

"Has not my hand made all these things, and so they came into being?" declares the LORD. "This is the one I esteem: he who is humble and contrite in spirit, and trembles at my word." (Isaiah 66:2)

"I have loved you with an everlasting love." (Jeremiah 31:3)

Therefore, there is now no condemnation for those who are in Christ Jesus . . . Who shall separate us from the love of Christ? Shall trouble or hardship or

*persecution or famine or nakedness or danger or sword? . . . No, in all these
things we are more than conquerors through him who loved us. For I am convinced that neither death nor life, neither angels nor demons, neither the present
nor the future, nor any powers, neither height nor depth, nor anything else in
all creation, will be able to separate us from the love of God that is in Christ
Jesus our Lord.* (Romans 8:1,35,37-39)

*For we are God's workmanship, created in Christ Jesus to do good works, which
God prepared in advance for us to do.* (Ephesians 2:10)

I can do everything through him who gives me strength. (Philippians 4:13)

*You are a chosen people, a royal priesthood, a holy nation, a people belonging to
God, that you may declare the praises of him who called you out of darkness into
his wonderful light.* (1 Peter 2:9)

If we endure, we will also reign with him. (2 Timothy 2:12)

- What is the most difficult thing about getting our "head knowledge" (about
who we are in God's eyes) to move down into our hearts?

Biblical Submission: It's Great!

Perhaps you've been thoroughly convinced about the nature of biblical submission.
You accept the idea that it's a mutual calling and that both you and your spouse
have significant parts to play. But now it's time to get more specific about what submission actually "looks like" in everyday life. We can do this by looking at two sets
of seemingly conflicting descriptions.

It's perceptive. We've already spoken about getting behind our spouse's eyes
and hearing his or her heart. It's all to say that biblical submission is a lifelong
process of learning and perceiving what things in life and love are the most mean-
ingful and satisfying to your spouse. I learn more about my wife Sande every year.
This is a woman who insists on balancing the checkbook. I don't understand why
she balances the checkbook. (To be honest, I don't even understand why anyone
writes down their check numbers, when the bank sends you a statement at the end
of the month telling you all about the checks you wrote.)

Anyway . . . Sande's one of these color-coordinated people who balances her
checkbook, likes *Country Living* magazine, and decorates with all kinds of cute

"country" items. For twelve years I've had to look at a country cow above the range in our kitchen, complete with a stenciled sign that reads, "Farm Fresh Milk." I've learned to accept that and be submissive to her. I look at it all and appreciate her decorating sense. I compliment her and encourage her creativity. (The good news is she seems to be tiring of the country look and moving toward that "shabby chic" look. Oh well, I can handle another change of décor.) Again, the point is: I learn to *see* what makes her happy, and then I highlight it, compliment it, and encourage it.

But it's blind, too. I got home one day and discovered that my wife had backed the van into our garage door. In fact, I would have to stoop low underneath the door to get in the house!

Krissy met me with, "What are you gonna do, Daddy?"

"Watch," I said.

I went in and found Sande in the kitchen.

"How was your day, Honey?" I asked, greeting her with a big smile.

"Oh, fine," she whispered. But I could see tears in her eyes.

"Let's go out to dinner," I said.

We all had to crawl underneath the door to get out to the car, but the damage was never mentioned. Krissy never knew that submission could be so blind. In other words, sometimes we need to look the other way, downplaying our spouse's mistakes, blunders, and shortcomings. We turn a blind eye so that we can preserve the relationship.

This all goes to say that submitting to our spouses means taking every opportunity to encourage and build them up. Sometimes that means *acknowledging* the "good"; at other times it means *ignoring* the "bad."

Individually consider each case below. In the spaces provided, mark an "S" or a "B," depending on the opportunity you think the event provides. Then, as a couple, go back and pick one "See" event that is closest to something you've experienced in the past. Together, develop a brief roleplay of a likely conversation that would take place in that event. Be as realistic as possible as you present this roleplay to the whole group.

SEEING OR BLINDED?

S = This is an opportunity to "See" (acknowledge the good).
B = This is an opportunity to be "Blind" (ignore the bad).

Husbands:
___ 1. Your wife announces that she's starting her own home-based business—again.
___ 2. You discover that your wife has forgotten to deduct a $200 ATM charge from the checkbook balance. You wonder whether the account is now overdrawn.

continued

___ 3. You come home late from work, and the house is completely dark. Entering the living room to turn on a lamp, you fall headlong over a small coffee table. Once the lights are on, you hobble through the rest of the rooms, rubbing your throbbing shin bones. Every piece of furniture in the house has been moved and rearranged!

___ 4. Your wife buys you a plaid shirt for your birthday. You hate plaid.

___ 5. Your wife surprises you with the "newest look" in hairstyles. To you, it appears she's gotten her head a little too close to the weed whacker.

Wives:

___ 1. Your husband announces that he's quit his job and is signing up for a career-development course.

___ 2. You come home from work to find that your husband has used the "good towels" for cleaning and waxing the kitchen floor. He has a very proud look on his face.

___ 3. Your husband has told you the office party is an "informal" affair. As you both walk into the room in jeans, you're quite surprised to find all the women in evening gowns—sitting next to men in tuxedoes.

___ 4. Your husband has just confessed to being attracted to his secretary at work. In fact, they have even kissed. "What should I do?" he asks fearfully.

___ 5. Your husband has made you dinner. As he serves the food, he's ultra-serious, wanting everything to be perfect—as if it were a sacred event. To you, the meal appears sacred, all right: partly burnt offering and partly bloody sacrifice!

It's romantic. I've made it a practice to take my wife to a local hotel about every six months. The first time I did this, Sande was automatically suspicious as we walked into this room with the king-size bed. Five sweetheart roses graced the nightstand.

I know what she thought.

You know what she thought.

I tucked her in bed. I gave her a book. I let her know that she would receive a wakeup call at noon the next day and I would pick her up at 1 P.M. Then I left her on her own, in a plush hotel room with a good book to read. Oh yes, one more thing. I ordered her a chocolate goody for dessert and made sure room service brought her a small pot of *fresh* coffee.

When I tell this story at conferences all the women sigh in unison. You never knew submission could be so romantic, did you?

But it's sacrificial, too. I always admired my friend Jerry Kindall's championship ring that he won while playing with the Minnesota Twins. Jerry was second baseman on the Twins team that won an American League pennant before he became the baseball coach at the University of Arizona, where we got acquainted. That gold ring—with its huge diamond imbedded in the center—was something Jerry wore proudly and frequently.[2]

One day several years ago I ran into his wife, Georgia, at church and noticed the diamond pendant she was wearing.

"Georgia, that's a beautiful pendant," I observed.

"Oh, didn't I tell you?" she responded. "My Jerry gave it to me."

Our eyes met. I knew where it came from.

"Not *The Ring?*" I said almost fearfully. Why had he sacrificed the ring?

Georgia affirmed that Jerry had indeed cut the diamond up to make a pendant for her and pins for his four children. At first I was incredulous, but as I thought about it, knowing Jerry, it sounded like something he would do.

Eventually I asked him about it. He told me that he decided to do it because he realized how blessed he was, especially by his family, and he wanted to share something with them that held great value to him.

Georgia died a few years later of Lou Gehrig's Disease. She died knowing that her husband cared enough about her to sacrifice one of his most treasured possessions—for someone he treasured even more. For me, that sacrifice will always be a poignant illustration of submission. Sacrificial submission never looked so good on anyone.

As you come to the close of this session, take a moment to talk with your spouse about the balance of romance and sacrifice in your marriage—two critical aspects of submission. Share your responses to the two questions below. Use the first question to spur you into making specific plans for romance. Use the second question as a launching pad for mutual expressions of gratitude and appreciation.

- What is the most romantic thing I could do for you in the weeks ahead?

- What is the most sacrificial thing you've noticed me doing during the years/months of our relationship/marriage?

Spend a little time sharing about some of the issues of submission in your marriage and family. What things could use some prayer? To close, everyone pray for the person on his or her right.

Keeping the Promise

1. Ask your spouse to make a list of ten things that would make you a better spouse. Read through it carefully—and then try to do some of the things on the list!

2. Look over the traits of a perfectionist and a pursuer of excellence on page 68. Circle the traits that are most true of you. Underline the traits that are true of your spouse. Discuss with your spouse ways you can encourage each other to become pursuers of excellence.

3. If you circled many perfectionist traits, ask your spouse: "In what area(s) of our marriage have I been most demanding?" Write his or her response on a note card and commit it to memory.

4. Memorize Ephesians 2:10. When your spouse is discouraged at some time during this week, repeat this verse to him or her.

5. Try this "He Said/She Said" discussion starter: How can Christian men and women communicate the biblical concept of submission to the world so that it is properly understood and not distorted?

Commitment Check

A Couple of Promise must *treasure each other as gifts from God.* In the space below, writing as if from behind God's eyes (and in His voice), describe what makes your spouse valuable to Him.

Answer key to "Perfectionists Everyone?" on pages 68-69:
If you checked two or less of the statements, you're probably only mildly perfectionist. If you checked half of them, you're moderately perfectionist. If you checked six to ten, you're not only too hard on yourself, but you're probably very hard on everyone around you!

Portions of this session were adapted from:

Leman, Kevin. *Winning the Rat Race Without Becoming a Rat* (Nashville, Tenn: Nelson, 1996), pages 138-139, 239-243. This includes the story about Jerry Kindall.

For further information, consider:

Wright, H. Norman. *Premarital Counseling.* Chicago: Moody Press, 1977. See the eight "Marriageability Traits" beginning on page 28.

Stoop, David. *Hope for the Perfectionist.* Nashville, Tenn.: Nelson, 1991.

NOTES

1. Kevin Leman, *Winning the Rat Race Without Becoming a Rat* (Nashville, Tenn.: Nelson, 1996), pp. 138-139.
2. Leman, *Winning the Rat Race. . . .*

"What's Wrong?" "Nothing!"

W hile speaking in Phoenix at a parochial school, I ate dinner that evening with the nuns. My wife was with me, and on the way home I noticed that Sande was being very quiet. "What's wrong?" I asked.

"Oh, nothing."

"Nothing?"

That's a typical conversation between a husband and wife. The conversation goes nowhere. Fortunately, Sande and I went beyond the "What's wrong? Oh, nothing" stage to delve into the root of the problem.

Which turned out to be me.

You see, we eventually cleared the air because I insisted that she communicate her true feelings, and in due time she did. Apparently I had been way too friendly with a nun from Spain.

As a supplement to this session, view "What's Wrong? . . . Nothing!" on the videotape "Keeping the Promise," Tape 1. Consider starting your session with the opening skit. Then ask your group members, "Why is it often so tough just to say what's on our minds in a marriage?"

The Challenge: Communicate!

Communication is probably the most overused word in our vocabulary today when we talk about marriage. Everybody knows we've got to communicate. But how do we learn to do it—and do it well? Most of us didn't grow up talking freely about our feelings, our hopes and fears, our deepest longings. We held these things in and kept them to ourselves. But these are exactly the things married couples need to be comfortable talking about if they're to grow in love and unity over the years. So why don't we do it very well?

Why Don't Couples Communicate?

In this day of enlightenment, most couples do want to communicate. But for a variety of reasons, they don't. Let's look at them.

"I just don't know how." Yes, we're talking ignorance here. Some couples are vastly uninformed about basic communication techniques and therefore fall prey to constant conflict . . . or enduring silence. For example, they may not know about a simple rule that helps tremendously when raising potential sore spots in a relationship: Use "I" statements instead of "You" statements. That is, rather than accusing your spouse ("Fred, you need to show more affection!"), it's better to share about yourself ("I'm feeling a need to be hugged a little more these days"). Who could argue with a statement about your need? Now Fred can decide what to do without having to feel put down.

The point is, if we're unaware of basic communication skills, we'll often choose the least effective alternatives for meeting our needs in the relationship. And there are many alternatives when it comes to how we communicate—especially when conflict looms. David Augsburger, in his book *Caring Enough to Confront*, lists them like this:

1. I win—you lose
2. I want out, I'll withdraw
3. I'll give in for good relations
4. I'll meet you halfway
5. I can care and confront

"The last [option] is the most effective," he says. It's "the most truly loving, the most growth-promoting for human relationships. But all five have their rightful place, their proper time of usage, their appropriate moment."[1]

However, not even knowing your options is a severe limitation! How informed are you?

"I'm so afraid." Many couples are afraid to tell each other the truth. How many times have you heard, or conducted, this conversation:

"How ya doin'?"

"I'm fine."

But I'm rarely tempted to say, "My hemorrhoids are killing me!"

We are especially great for this kind of small-talk exchange in the church. We start off with sentences like "This is the day that the Lord has made, let us rejoice

Note-it

Attention all husbands! Your wife can't keep your family together all by herself. You must play an active role in helping sort out the urgent and the important—and then do your share of both.

and be glad in it." Yet four minutes earlier, we'd been screaming at our child, "Get in the car! Now!" You see, *we're afraid to reveal how things really are for us because we have an appearance to maintain, a mask we've put on to keep others from getting too close.* But as Nathaniel Hawthorne once said, "No man, for any considerable period, can wear one face to himself and another to the multitude without finally getting bewildered as to which may be the true." Let's admit it: our secret fear is that if people really discovered who we are they might conclude that they don't like what they've found.

"It's way too tough." For some couples, it seems like too much trouble to deepen the communication level. There are so many other things to do with our time. There are so many pressing demands, so many tempting opportunities—other than to just sit and communicate with each other. It takes a certain amount of discipline and courage to say, "No, at this particular moment it's more important for me to stop, look directly into my spouse's eyes, and invite a clearing of the air." Those are the precious times when we choose the best for our spouse over the seemingly urgent call to meet our own needs. When was the last time you laid everything else aside just to say, "Now what, exactly, is on your mind, Honey?"

"Boy, am I discouraged!" Okay, maybe you've tried and tried, with little success. Maybe your spouse shows little interest in better communication. Or maybe you've given it your best shot and things still haven't improved. If you were raised with the understanding that kids should "speak only when spoken to," perhaps you took that questionable bit of worldly wisdom and made it an airtight rule for your adult communication patterns as well. In any case, you're thoroughly discouraged. And you aren't talking about it.

"Huh? What?" Pure inattention can be the problem. Here I refer to a common situation among married couples: forgetting the basic male-female differences in approaching communication. For example, did you know that women are *accumulators;* men are *terminators?* It's been reported that women use almost four times the words that men use. They tend to keep adding to the conversation, so it keeps on going.

The male instinct, on the other hand, is to end a conversation quickly. It goes back to that fix-it mentality. The apostle James must have understood something about terminator tendencies when he wrote, "Everyone should be quick to listen, slow to speak" (James 1:19).

Note-it

This week would be a good time to review the story of Samson and Delilah in Judges 16. Once you've read this powerful chapter, focus on Samson's desire to terminate his ill-fated conversation with Delilah beginning in verse 6. That desire ended his own life too soon!

Think about how different things might have been if Samson had taken the time to discuss at length how God had blessed him with such strength. Suppose he had revealed the nature of his own relationship with God? Weary of Delilah's repeated questioning, however, Samson terminated the conversation with the bare facts. Delilah accumulated his hair, and Samson himself got . . . terminated.

Men, fight the urge to be who you are! Take the time to listen. If you really want to develop communication skills, take a tip from the business world. How many of your companies send you places to learn to be better listeners? Start by noticing the tone of voice your wife is using and respond to that. The feelings she's communicating are just as important—or more so?—as the words.

Wives, don't ask your husbands "Why?" so often. Using the word "why" too frequently puts your husband on the defensive. Instead say, "Tell me more about that" or "I'd like to hear more."

Quickly review the five typical reasons for not communicating well in a marriage. Then take these three steps:

Step 1: Separately, identify yourself on the scale below by circling where you think you are in relation to each of the five reasons. (The 1 at the left means "no ability" and the 10 at the right means "great ability.") Then place a mark where you think you would like to be. Finally, place an "S" where you think your spouse is.

Step 2: Separately, name one specific area in your marriage in which you'd like to improve your communication.

Step 3: Together, compare your responses in steps 1 and 2 above. Then analyze your desired "improvement area" (from step 2). Decide which of the five non-communication reasons is at the heart of your lack of communication in this area. Then discuss the two questions at the end of this exercise.

RATE YOURSELF:
REASONS FOR NOT COMMUNICATING

	No ability to overcome it								Great ability to overcome it
Ignorance	1	2	3	4	5	6	7	8	9	10
Fear	1	2	3	4	5	6	7	8	9	10
Difficulty	1	2	3	4	5	6	7	8	9	10
Discouragement	1	2	3	4	5	6	7	8	9	10
Inattention	1	2	3	4	5	6	7	8	9	10

■ I'd like to see us improve our communication in this area:

His response:

Her response:

1. How can we overcome this barrier in the future?

2. What is the next step for us in this area?

What Level of Communication Do You Seek?

Jesuit priest John Powell, who wrote *Why Am I Afraid to Tell You Who I Am?* identifies several levels of communication.[2]

Level One: Having a clichéd conversation. This is conversation at its most superficial level. For example, you ask: "Dear, have you seen my shoes?" She responds: "Look in the closet." It's an important level, and it takes up a large volume of our words each day. We use it to keep things running smoothly. But it has little affect on strengthening the relationship.

Level Two: Reporting facts about other people and events. Couples are great at this. We can spend hours discussing who did what, with whom, when, and why. But when

Note-it

Couples, it's possible to work at developing your communication skills together during the week. Try an exercise like this at home: Sit in chairs facing each other. One partner starts off by saying something at the feeling level. Communicate directly, eyeball to eyeball. The other person's responsibility is just to listen. Try not to think about what to say back in return. Then the listening spouse should communicate back what was said. Allow for clarifications. This is a simple, but effective, way to stimulate deeper levels of conversation.

do you discuss your own relationship? Level two conversations keep you from talking about the things you need to talk about as a couple.

Level Three: Exchanging ideas and opinions. Most of us spend too much time at level two and too little time discussing our ideas and judgments. Interchanges don't always have to be gut wrenching. There is a place in marriage for an exchange of views—the right hand has to know what the left hand is doing.

You must talk, for example, about roles in marriage. I kiddingly say my wife is the mechanic in our family. I'm not mechanical. Actually, this year I've committed to memorizing the names of the tools so when she needs something I'll know which one to give her! She's the one who fixes things, and we talk about the best ways to proceed on any given project. But at some point in a healthy marriage we must talk about our feelings and emotions, too.

Level Four: Sharing feelings and needs. This is the level we want to strive toward. At this level we are saying, "I feel this way." We are sending those "I" messages referred to earlier. Remember: *Feelings will draw you together; judgments will drive you apart.* If you're feeling distance in your marriage, it's likely because there's too much judgment flying around.

Guess who's great at spouting edicts and judgments?

Men.

They are fixers by nature (but not necessarily with tools). Women come to them with a problem and they're going to fix it. Most women, however, aren't interested in husbands telling them how to solve the problem. They simply want their man to listen, to validate the pain a problem is causing, and to offer comfort in the midst of it all. They want their husbands to understand. When a man comes home from work, guess what his wife sees? She sees relief! He, of course, wants to sit down and read the paper. Will he choose to listen closely to feelings and needs?

Level Five: Risking complete emotional and personal truthfulness. This level is the most difficult to reach, but it's worth it. You've really got to be vulnerable and trusting. When you share some intimate thought or desire, you're really saying to your mate, "I trust you."

Complete the following matching exercise by jotting the letter of a statement in the blanks next to the five communication levels. (Hint: There is more than one statement for some of the types of communication.)

When you're finished matching, go back to each of the first four levels and change their matching statement(s) so that the communication level is moved up one notch. (For example, "It's raining!" [level 2] might change to "I think it's supposed to rain more this year" [level 3].) Then form small groups to share your new statements.

Finally, discuss this question: How can we move our communication levels "up the scale" in everyday conversation with our spouses?

— 1. Clichéd conversation	a. "Right now, I'm really wishing my mom were still alive."
__ 2. Reporting facts	b. "I heard that Bob, Carol, Ted, and Alice are going on a ski trip next month."
__ 3. Exchanging ideas/opinions	c. "Say, what did you think about Smith's editorial in the *Journal* this morning?"
__ 4. Sharing feelings/needs	d. "Nice weather, isn't it, Dear?"
	e. "Just watching the kid turn a double play brings tears to my eyes."
__ 5. Risking complete personal truthfulness	f. "I'm not sure why, but I'm having trouble getting interested in sex these days."
	g. "Good morning, Sugar Dumplin! How ya doin'?"
	h. "The thing is, I know we all have to die. But the thought sure is scaring me."

As a couple, consider the discussion questions below. (Note: If time is short in your group, plan to talk about these questions during the coming week.)

1. At which communication level do you and your spouse spend the most time?

1   2   3   4   5

(Circle one)

2. How often would you say you move to the deepest level?

___ frequently
___ occasionally
___ rarely
___ never

Give an example:

When we . . .

3. What do you do when you feel frustrated in your attempts at deeper levels of communication?

4. What are the most helpful things to do?

Which Rules Are You Using?

Most of us carry around some guidelines—mostly unspoken—about how we ought to communicate with our spouses. We have some definite ideas about what is appropriate and what is good in a marital conversation. But let's get more specific about a few standard rules that anyone can apply in order to foster good communication.

Don't go to bed mad. You'll find this bit of common-sense advice clearly stated in the Bible: "In your anger do not sin. Do not let the sun go down while you are still angry" (Ephesians 4:26).

In other words, a mad bed is a bad bed. If there's something bothering you, it's best to get it out on the table as soon as possible. Going to bed with bitterness and frustration only keeps tensions running high in the marriage. And if held in over a long period of time, when the problem does finally surface it's more likely to gush out in a dam burst of accusation and personal attack. That's just not necessary.

Keep your feelings warm. One day two ice fishermen were out trying their luck. The young guy watched the senior citizen pulling up fish after fish through the small hole in the ice. The young man yelled over to the old-timer, "What's your secret?"

He mumbled something back.

"I said, 'What's your secret?'"

He mumbled again.

"What?"

The elderly man then spit out a small, brown, wiggly mass into his hand. "You gotta keep your worms warm!"[3]

In the same fashion, I'm here to suggest: You've got to keep feelings warm in a marriage. Don't let them go stale. Even if you've got conflicts, work them out together passionately. It's always better to be fully engaged than to clam up and walk away from each other—either physically or emotionally.

Deal directly with anger. First, it's important to recognize that anger is a valid emotion. We can't just say to ourselves: *Don't feel that way.* When anger is there, it's there. The issue is how we handle it and what we do with it. Go back and reread Ephesians 4:26. The apostle Paul has no problem recognizing that anger will occur. In fact, you'll recall that Jesus got angry. He charged the temple and overturned the tables of the moneychangers in a fit of righteous rage (see John 2:12-25).

Remember, however, this was the same man who preached turning the other cheek. Just as Ecclesiastes 3 declares that there is a time for every purpose under the heavens, there is a time to turn the other cheek and also a time to pull the rug out from under the one who's attempting to avoid personal responsibility for wrong actions. Our anger can spur us to confront problems head-on, keeping responsibility where it belongs.

While validating anger and action, Ephesians 4:26 also warns us about the potential for sinning in the midst of such strong feelings. Putting a lid on our anger, letting it go stale, so to speak, instead of keeping it warm and dealing with it right at the proper time, can actually open us up to sin.

Learn to fight fair. Properly communicating with each other allows us the opportunity to work through problems and conflicts. And be assured: conflict hits every marriage—regularly.

When you face conflict with your spouse, do you fight fair? Many psychologists and counselors talk about fair and unfair fighting techniques. In the exercise below, you'll explore a few of the most common unfair tactics.

Once you think you've got a handle on the descriptions of the six unfair fighting tactics below, begin thinking through your history of conflicts with your spouse. See if you can come up with an example of at least three of these unfair methods that you've used. Be ready to share your examples with your spouse during the week ahead. But also be sure to focus on how you can avoid being unfair with each other in the future! (Note: You might commit to calling out the tactic name whenever either of you slips into using one of them.)

SIX UNFAIR FIGHTING TACTICS

Universalizing: Making an unwarranted leap from a specific situation to a vast generalization. (Often makes use of "always" and "never.")

Example: "You're holding the garage sale *tomorrow?* Women are all alike—they never take the time to plan things out in a logical, organized way."

- A way I've used this tactic in the past (describe the situation):

continued

Character killing: Switching from the issues of the conflict to making a personal attack on your spouse. (May include sarcasm for a more devastating effect.)

Example: "Oh yeah? I think it's pretty obvious you're not exactly a Wall Street genius when it comes to handling the family's finances!"

▪ A way I've used this tactic in the past (describe the situation):

Cloud-covering: Making a vague, foggy accusation instead of being detailed and specific about a complaint. (Again, sarcasm helps!)

Example: "Hmmm . . . so I'm going to have the pleasure of enjoying your driving again? That should be . . . *interesting.*"

▪ A way I've used this tactic in the past (describe the situation):

Upping the ante: Instead of responding to the hurt or anger of your spouse, you just play "tit-for-tat" by citing a worse case that's been done to you.

Example: "You think forgetting your birthday is bad? What about when you forgot my graduation?"

▪ A way I've used this tactic in the past (describe the situation):

Scatter-bombing: Overwhelming your spouse with a barrage of faults and misdeeds that land all over the map. Dropping into the conversation a huge list of sins (usually unrelated)—including everything *and* the kitchen sink!

Example: "Yes, I may have been wrong. But you've been late before, and you bought all those tools without asking me, and remember you forgot to bring milk home yesterday, and you insulted my mother just last week, plus you quit your job that time, and furthermore . . ."

▪ A way I've used this tactic in the past (describe the situation):

continued

Moth-balling: Putting an old grievance in storage—for years or decades—and bringing it out at just the right time to hurt your spouse.

Example: "You think *I* hurt *you?* Well, Sally, I hate to bring it up, but remember the time back in 1986 when you had that little so-called 'business function' with Harry?"

▪ A way I've used this tactic in the past (describe the situation):

Spitting in your soup: Using passive-aggressive comments to lay the guilt on the other party. Often involves sarcasm.

Example: "No problem; you guys go ahead and play your sixty-four holes of golf. Have a great time! I'll just stay home and take care of Mom."

▪ A way I've used this tactic in the past (describe the situation):

One general rule to keep in mind: The best communication will always go after the problem, not the person. Find a place—the Jacuzzi, the breakfast table, or your patio, for example—to talk about the problem. I always tell people who are fighting to take their clothes off, get in the bathtub, and hold hands. You'd be surprised how difficult it is to fight while holding each other, no barriers between you, when the door is locked and you're by yourselves. It becomes a lot easier to get things on the table. And if you have the willingness in your heart, just listening to your partner makes all the difference in the world.

Let Love Do Its Work in the Midst of Anger. Read 1 Corinthians 13:4-8 again:

> *Love is patient, love is kind. It does not envy, it does not boast, it is not proud. It is not rude, it is not self-seeking, is not easily angered, it keeps no record of wrongs. Love does not delight in evil but rejoices with the truth. It always protects, always trusts, always hopes, always perseveres. Love never fails.*

This Scripture reassures us that love is not easily angered. But have you ever thought about why? Consider again the phrase that follows the not-easily-angered declaration: "It keeps no record of wrongs." In other words, no moth-balling allowed! When spouses lovingly refuse to keep a record of wrongs by dealing with problems and feelings as they occur, they aren't primed for anger. They aren't simmering, seething pots ready to boil over with the next provocation.

Let's continue with this train of thought. Read this passage of Scripture from Ephesians 4:29-32:

> *Do not let any unwholesome talk come out of your mouths, but only what is helpful for building others up according to their needs, that it may benefit those who listen. And do not grieve the Holy Spirit of God, with whom you were sealed for the day of redemption. Get rid of all bitterness, rage and anger, brawling and slander, along with every form of malice. Be kind and compassionate to one another, forgiving each other, just as in Christ God forgave you.*

Clearly the words in 1 Corinthians 13 and Ephesians 4:29-32 back up what we've been saying about good communication and fair fighting. In small groups, continue to talk through the implications of these Scripture passages. Use any of the following questions to get your discussion started.

1. In light of these Scriptures, what would you say is the highest purpose of communication?

2. What unfair fighting tactics could you connect to words and/or phrases in these passages? What forms of good communication could you connect?

3. What would it mean for a spouse to "delight in evil"?

4. How would you describe "kindness" in a marriage?

5. How do you think someone can go about getting rid of bitterness and anger? Do you believe that talking about problems can help you get rid of anger? What other ways do you find helpful?

6. Is there a difference between communicating feelings of anger and "brawling" or "slander"? Explain.

The Children: Tell 'em the Truth!

It's easy for any of us to stray from truthfulness or sincerity in our relationships. And that goes for relating to our children, too. Have you ever used evasive or deliberately vague language with them? Are you guilty of that with your children when it comes to conveying what married life is all about?

What Are You Telling Your Children?

It takes two steps to stop the charade (as well intentioned as it may be): being honest first with yourself, and then attempting complete honesty with your child.

Are you honest with yourself about the true nature of married life? We've already talked about unrealistic expectations. About how reality hits. What about the expectations you carry in your "mind talk," the internal conversation that's always chattering away? Is it honest?

My wife once sent me on an errand we men always thoroughly enjoy. I had to go to the store to purchase feminine products for her. Of course, I ended up buying the wrong kind. So I went back to the store and, in an effort to avoid any more embarrassment, I bought every kind they had. I was checked out by a young clerk, about nineteen years old, wearing four flesh-piercing earrings.

"Would you like a bag, sir?"

I wanted to say, "No, I'd like to stand here with all this stuff for another ten minutes."

It struck me later that this is just a part of marriage. What loving husband hasn't been to the store to buy his wife feminine products? But no one ever warned me about this aspect of marital bliss. No one bothered to communicate the whole story. Yet I can work on *keeping my expectations of married life realistic.* I can revel in the joys—*and* be ready to accept the challenges.

Are you honest with your children about the "real" married life? As you're dealing with your own expectations, what things do you communicate to your kids about marriage?

When it comes to this kind of direct honesty about married life, I think about the time when my daughter Holly was engaged and had gone to visit with her fiancé and his family over Christmas break. She heard Drew in the middle of the night and he was "sicker than a dog." She ended up taking care of him for about three hours straight through the middle of the night. As hard as that experience was for her, it went a long way toward preparing her for "real" married life. And it had a humorous side for me a couple days later when she said to me on the phone: "Dad, we're so glad we went to hear your talk about what real love is all about—with you telling all those 'hurling' examples!" (Remember my high-school talk in session 2?)

It's true that our married love must be able to enjoy the good times and endure the most difficult of circumstances. And yes, sometimes it's the hurling episodes that show us just how committed we are to the object of our love. That kind of scenario is closer to reality than what we're often telling our kids about marriage.

We've looked at many ideas in this session about how to communicate better—all for the purpose of building a stronger marriage. How do these ideas compare with our society's overall approach? What better way to check than by considering a few quotations from *Reader's Digest?* That's where you're likely to find the "man on the street" view.

In small groups (each without spouses, if possible), consider one of the following quotes about marriage and family. Then answer these questions for each one:

- To what extent do you agree with this quote?

- What personal illustration from your life seems to affirm or deny what's being said here?

- How would you say it to make it more relevant to a situation in your marriage or family life right now?

- If you could add one thing to this quote, what would it be?

- What key ideas here would you deem worthy to convey to your children (or warn them!) about marriage?

1. The family is not one of several alternative lifestyles; it is not an arena in which rights are negotiated; it is not an old-fashioned barrier to a promiscuous sex life; it is not a set of cost-benefit calculations. It is a commitment for which there is no feasible substitute. No child ought to be brought into a world where that commitment—from both parents—is absent.

   There is no way to prepare for the commitment other than to make it. Living together is not a way of finding out how married life will be, because married life is shaped by the fact that the couple has made a solemn vow before their family and friends that this is for keeps and that any children will be their joint and permanent responsibility. It changes everything.—James Q. Wilson[4]

2. Marriage is like a three-speed gearbox: affection, friendship, love. It is not advisable to crash your gears and go right through to love straightaway. You need to ease your way through. The basis of love is respect, and that needs to be learned from affection and friendship.
—Peter Ustinov[5]

Note-it

Sometimes couples don't know how to communicate the goodness of their marriage to their children. You'd like to say so many things about your life together, about the tough times and about the blessings.

Here's a suggestion: Make a video. In this day and age almost anybody can make a video. (Get someone to help if you're technologically challenged!) Talk about what's important in life. Recount your spiritual pilgrimage. Share from your heart. Like John Powell, ask yourself, "Why am I afraid to tell you who I really am?"

3. When a marriage matures, you can tolerate differences in each other. If she's social and he's a couch potato, it's okay for her to go out socially and for him to be home watching the ball game. Each one is happy that the other is having a good time; and neither one resents the other.

   That's generous love. Selfish love is when she drags him out or he keeps her home. But that's not really love: that's control. It takes generous love to survive the large and small events of a long relationship. It takes generous love to keep on listening to each other—and to learn from each other.—Daniel Gottlieb[6]

To close your session, focus on one key prayer concern of the group or of a group member. All of you pray about that concern, and commit to continuing your prayers during the coming week.

Keeping the Promise

1. Set aside fifteen minutes every day this week for uninterrupted conversation with your spouse about the themes in this session. Even if it feels as if the conversation is forced, try to express your thoughts and feelings to your spouse using statements that begin with "I feel" rather than "You always." Count how many times you use "I" statements in this conversation. Then plan to jot the number of "I" statements for each day of the coming week:

   Sunday _____
   Monday _____
   Tuesday _____
   Wednesday _____
   Thursday _____
   Friday _____
   Saturday _____

   Did your numbers decrease as the week progressed?

2. Practice becoming a better listener this week. Before responding to your spouse, repeat what you just heard him or her say. This will ensure that you heard your spouse correctly. At the end of the week, ask your spouse if you've remembered to do this repeating exercise.

3. Write a love letter to your spouse. Communicate all the positive benefits of your relationship.

4. Make a video for your kids that communicates the truths about marriage. In the video, be sure to recount your spiritual journey and your hopes for your children's own marriages.

5. "He Said/She Said" discussion starter: What does truthfulness actually mean? How can we communicate it as a value in society?

Commitment Check

Couples of Promise commit themselves to showing respect for each other, publicly and privately. Ask your spouse if there have been times when you've embarrassed him or her with words or actions (perhaps without realizing it).

> **Suggested responses to the communication-level matching exercise on page 83**: 1. d, g; 2. b; 3. c; 4. a, e; 5. f, h.

For further information, consider:

Rush, Myron. *Hope for Hurting Relationships.* Colorado Springs, Colo.: ChariotVictor Books, 1989. See especially the four "relationship styles," beginning on page 37.

Wright, H. Norman. *Communication: Key to Your Marriage.* Glendale, Calif.: Regal, 1974.

NOTES

1. David Augsburger, *Caring Enough to Confront* (Glendale, Calif.: Regal, 1976).
2. John Powell, *Why Am I Afraid to Tell You Who I Am?* (New York: Tabor Publishing, 1995). The five levels are from Powell; the commentary on them is mine.
3. This joke was told on the "Johnny Carson Show" by Burt Mustin. It's reported that it got the longest laugh in the show's history!
4. James Q. Wilson, in "Commentary," *Reader's Digest,* March 1996.
5. Peter Ustinov, in "Points to Ponder," *Reader's Digest,* October 1992.
6. Daniel Gottlieb, in "Points to Ponder," *Reader's Digest,* December 1991.

Her Needs and His

We live in an age of pervasive knowledge, seemingly boundless power, and enough intricate technology to put machinery on Mars. They tell us that soon we'll be sending faxes through our watches! We've all seen fantastic technological advances in every area of our lives. In this day of enlightenment, however, we men still don't understand women, and women don't understand men. How can that be?

It has to do with one little word: *needs.*

All marriages revolve around needs. And your marriage will succeed or fail depending on how good you are at discerning and meeting the true needs of your spouse. For example, both men and women want affection and sex (and women—physically—actually have the ability to enjoy sex much more than men). But men and women have unique needs in terms of what "fulfilling" affection and sex means for them. That's why husbands and wives must work so hard at meeting the needs of their spouses. In the process, they'll likely find their own needs being fulfilled.

As a supplement to this session, view "Her Needs and His" on the videotape "Keeping the Promise," Tape 2. If you wish, launch this session by playing the opening skit on this section of the tape. Then invite your participants to name some of the differences between "exchanging information" and "communication." Do they have any personal evidence that men and women view this issue differently?

Recognizing Those Needs

A woman's needs and a man's needs are very, very different. So let's take a look at how we want our spouses to respond to those differences. First, of course, we'll simply have to become aware of our distinctions and understand our unique needs. After that, we can work on meeting one another's needs to enhance this relationship we call married life.

> God help the man who won't marry until he finds a perfect woman, and God help him still more if he finds her.
>
> —Benjamin Tillett

Understanding His Needs

Ladies, try answering this question: What is a married man's primary need in marriage?

Did you guess admiration and encouragement? Is it communication? Sex? Food?

Most women really believe they have us men figured out. But they're wrong. They think the answer to that question is "sex." It's not. It's "sexual fulfillment" (more about that in a moment). And that little distinction makes a huge difference from behind a man's eye. And women also need to get behind a man's eyes to understand his needs. Let's look at three of the most basic needs for men in marriage.

To be respected. Respecting your husband has to do with honoring his ideals, his goals, and his dreams. It means a pat on the back for his good motives when he works hard for the family. It means giving him the benefit of the doubt when he's had to take the lead in making tough decisions for the good of the family. In all of these things, his deepest values are going to shine through. So the big question is: Can you learn to value what he values? (I'm assuming here that he's seeking to follow the Lord.)

Respect also has a lot to do with keeping family matters inside the family. For instance, we men don't think it's a good idea for wives to tell their girlfriends, mothers, or sisters about our marriages. We want what goes on between us to stay between us. That's how most men think. So, wives, resist the urge to pull the prayer chain on your husband's behalf. He wants you to respect his privacy. Ask him. He's going to tell you to button it up. Remember, we men are terminators. We like things in their little cubicles.

One assumption in what I'm saying here about respect flows from a simple, all-important guideline for relationships: "Treat people like persons, not things." Spouses guilty of seeing their mates as workhorses or sex objects are violating this principle.

Quickly turn to your spouse for a little chat. First, ask your spouse if there are ever times when he or she feels like a workhorse or a sex object. Jot your responses in the blanks that follow. Then take a moment to complete the partial sentence at the end of this exercise. Briefly discuss your responses. (Be sure to cite an example or two that shows what "being respected" means to you, in practical terms.)

- His response:

- Her response:

- I know I'm truly being respected by my spouse when . . .

To be needed. A man wants to feel needed by his wife. He wants to know that he's the number-one priority in his wife's life in terms of human relationships. Yet many a man feels as though he's landed in second place compared to his wife's interest in the relationships attached to her roles as employee, homemaker, and mother. Wives need to realize, therefore, that inside that man is a little boy who needs to know he's loved and prized for who he is.

It's true that there's been a feminization of men over the years, and some women see that as a good thing. (Before long the men will be throwing Tupperware parties and eating quiche on a regular basis.) Yet I've never had a woman come into my office and say, "I love my husband's effeminate nature." Nor have I ever had a man come in and confide, "I love my wife's masculinity. She's tough as nails." Despite intense pressure from society, this unisex ideal is not what our spouses want or need. Maybe God the Creator had a great idea, after all: the masculine and feminine—so unique and differing—could come together and make great music, because they complement and complete each other so perfectly.

To be sexually fulfilled. I don't know where we got this idea that men only want physical sexual satisfaction. As a man married for thirty-two years, I get much more psychological, emotional pleasure out of watching my wife enjoy me than from my own physical satisfaction. Fulfillment comes in the exploration and enjoyment of our sexual *complementarity*. For a man, this involves feeling completely accepted by his wife while he's in his most vulnerable, "naked" state—as a man. She loves him with all of his fears, flaws, and foibles. She perfectly accepts his ways of loving and lets him know that he is the greatest. Then his enjoyment is complete.

In this regard, I think of Proverbs 5:18: "May you rejoice in the wife of your youth." What do you think the writer meant by "rejoice"? Sex is a gift from Almighty God. Celebrating our sexual and emotional *differences*—which leads to sexual fulfillment—allows us to have a great marriage. (And by the way, don't forget companionship. You are lovers, but work at becoming best friends, too.)

Form two groups, one for the men and one for the women. Women, consider the case of Rhonda; men, the case of Jim. You are the best friend—and it's time to respond! Do two things: (1) define what you think is the "problem" and (2) brainstorm a list of possible "first steps" a friend might suggest.

Rhonda said to her best friend: "You know, Jim and I have sex quite a bit, and physically, it's fine. But I'm thinking there's got to be more to it. I mean, on the fulfillment side. Somehow, it's not that satisfying just to go through the motions. Do you know what I'm trying to say?"

Jim confided to his best friend: "Talking about sex, do you ever get the feeling that it should be better? I mean, I'm not talking just about the physical act, and I'm certainly not looking for somebody else besides Rhonda. I'm just thinking that it shouldn't have to become so routine after a few years of marriage. Am I missing something?"

- Define the "problem":

- Suggest some "first steps" that Rhonda or Jim could take:

Now find your spouse and move to a private place in the room or building. Discuss the case of Rhonda and Jim above. Also talk about the ideas raised among the men and women in your separate groups. After a few minutes, consider the two questions below. Take plenty of time to discuss your responses.

- What are the missing elements that make "sex" into "sexual fulfillment" in marriage?

- Are there any missing elements in our relationship these days?

In session 2, we looked briefly at some passages in 1 Corinthians. Now let's review what Paul has told us in chapter 7 verses 3-5:

> *The husband should fulfill his marital duty to his wife, and likewise the wife to her husband. The wife's body does not belong to her alone but also to her husband. In the same way, the husband's body does not belong to him alone but also to his wife. Do not deprive each other except by mutual consent and for a time, so that you may devote yourselves to prayer. Then come together again so that Satan will not tempt you because of your lack of self-control.*

After considering the instructions in 1 Corinthians 7:3-5, how would you answer the following questions?

- In light of this passage, is it permissible for husbands and wives to abstain from sex?

- According to the Scripture, does a period of abstention from sexual relations have restrictions? How long should a period of abstention last?

- For what reason cited may a husband and wife decide to abstain?

- Who decides to initiate the period of abstention?

- Suppose one partner resists a period of abstention? What counsel do you think Paul would give?

Let these ideas sink in: The man should give his body to his wife; a woman doesn't have full rights over her own body. Try selling that one to the media today! I interpret this passage as saying that my wife's body belongs to me—and mine to her—and it doesn't get violated with any other person. And if we do separate for anything (the Bible says for prayer), then we come back together soon.

I just love the apostle Paul. He's wonderfully direct and specific. I hope that by studying his instructions, you've come to realize that sex is not only a wonderful privilege of marriage, but also a requirement for nurturing a healthy marital relationship.

Understanding Her Needs

Men, what's the number one need for a married woman? If you guessed "a VISA card," you're wrong. Here are the top three needs of women in a marriage.

The need for affection. This is not the same as sex, an important distinction that most males need to note. And it brings up an important point, too—about a man's tendency to "grab." In any crowded room we'll probably find men who are world-class grabbers. Women don't like to be grabbed. At the risk of sounding redundant, let me repeat it. I've asked this question everywhere, and the answer's always the same: Women don't like to be grabbed. They like to be held, petted, and patted—gently—but they don't like to be grabbed. You've got to use the good brain that God gave you and realize that love always has limits and that discipline is part of it. If there's no discipline to love, there can be no love in the relationship.

My whole idea here is based on the fact that men and women are different physically. You noticed? For example, how long does it take a husband to get interested in sex? Six seconds, and he's ready. How long does it take the wife? Forty-seven minutes. You see the problem. Counselor and writer Gary Smalley has said that men are like microwaves and women are like crockpots. How true.

Understanding how different we are makes all the difference in the world. Another writer on marriage, Willard Harley, has said that when it comes to sex and affection, you can't have one without the other. Again, how true. When men and women bring their differences to the marriage relationship, the result must be a careful balance.

The need for honesty and openness. We've seen that men typically offer short answers, but women want to talk. Yet we men carry around a lot of fear, the fear of vulnerability that comes with conversations that go to a deeper level than mere weather reporting. Here's how men's writer James B. Nelson put it:

> Underneath all explanations for men's difficulty in friendship I believe there lies one pervasive and haunting theme: *fear.* Fear of vulnerability. Fear of our emotions. Fear of being uncovered, found out. So my fear leads to my desire to control—to be in control of situations, to be in control of my feelings, to be in control of my relationships. Then I will be safe. No one will really know my weakness and my vulnerability. No one will really know my doubts. No one will really know that I am not the producer and achiever I seem to be. Therein lies my real terror.[1]

In spite of the fear, consider the great benefits of risking realness with our wives. We'll take a huge load off of our shoulders, guys. We'll free up so much energy—the sheer effort it takes to keep everything so tightly bound up inside. And we'll likely discover that so much of what we've been holding in is of little concern to our wives. So much of what we fear revealing—for fear of rejection—will be perfectly accepted by them. And if something in us needs to change, then they'll be more than willing to help. Yet how will we ever know, unless we take the risk of talking?

Proverbs 25:11 lets us know that we can give our spouses a very valuable gift when we take time to communicate honestly, openly, and meaningfully with them. During a minute of silence, let the imagery of this verse (printed below) wash over you. Then silently answer the questions that follow.

A word aptly spoken is like apples of gold in settings of silver (Proverbs 25:11).

- What kind of visual image springs to mind from this verse?

- Could you see yourself delivering to your spouse a gift of "gold" in a "silver box" when you truly communicate with him or her? What would that mean, in practical terms?

- When was the last time you said something like this to your spouse: "Dear, you are my richest blessing"? How do you think he or she would respond?

- What gold-and-silver things would you like to say to your spouse today?

The need for commitment to the family. Wives like it when we love whom they love. Her brother, for example, may be the village idiot. But he's still her brother.

This applies to loving the children, as she loves the children. When my daughter Holly received an acceptance letter from Grove City College, I ordered a bouquet of sweetheart flowers to be delivered to her at our house. Because I was out of town and it was the day before Valentine's Day, her first thought upon accepting the bouquet from the delivery person was that it was intended for Sande.

Note-it

Don't forget . . .
All marriages revolve around a short but very big word—needs.
   Husbands and wives have basic but not similar needs that must be fulfilled by their mate.
   Men and women both want great sex and affection. Generally speaking, men want more sex and women desire more affection, but the reverse also can be true.
   Women want their husbands to anticipate their needs in advance, not after the fact.
   The typical wife seldom gets enough hugs. She can always use another hug—and another and another.[2]

"These are for you, Holly," Sande told her, showing her the card.

Holly took the flowers, now thinking they were from a boyfriend. She recalled the scene for me when I phoned later that day.

"But, Daddy, it was even better than that," she said. "They were from *you.*"

What do you think Sande Leman was thinking at that point?

It goes back to what I've already said: Women ask men every day, "Do you really love me?" When a husband meets her needs for affection, honesty, and openness, and gives evidence that he's committed to her family, she feels loved. If, on the other hand, all a man seems to be interested in from behind a wife's eyes is sex, then she's going to feel used. Let me remind you that marriage is not a 50/50 proposition. It's a 100/100 venture. Marriage ought to be a giving situation. We have to be willing to meet each other's needs.

 Spouses, take a moment to mark your "identity" from among the choices below. Then talk it over!

When it comes to telling my spouse what I need for a fulfilling relationship, I'd have to say I'm:

___ Pacifist Pat: I'd rather be quiet and keep the peace than bring up a deep need that might send us to battle stations.

___ Kickin' Kim: If I don't like it, I'll definitely let you know—right now!

___ Cruise-Control Chris: I'm content to continue down the road, at a steady pace, with things just as they are.

___ Jivin' Jamie: I might fake it a little bit, just to keep things cool, you know?

___ Klosed-up Kelly: How could you ask such a question?

___ Rappin' Robin: Yeah, Baby. Let's talk. No problemo—as long as we get it all out on the table.

___ Other:

Enhancing the Relationship

In his great book *The Five Love Languages,* Gary Chapman describes the key ways we feel and express love.[3] If you want to truly love your spouse, you need to understand his or her personal love languages. Here are the options:

1. Physical touch
2. Acts of service
3. Words of affirmation
4. Gifts
5. Quality time

How do these look in real life? Well, imagine a woman who's having dinner guests and wants to offer some little cookies to depict Valentine's Day—cookies with those traditional sayings on them like "Be Mine" and "You're My One Love." She wants to tie them up in a little bag with a ribbon as a place setting at each chair around the table. Her love language is to offer "acts of service." That's just how this woman sees life. When people are coming to her house, she wants to make sure they're entertained and feel welcome. She likes to do things special and different.

Now her husband has a different love language. He's a "quality time" person and he's upstairs wishing his wife would come and watch the football or hockey game with him. So he's yelling down the stairs, "Hey, Honey! When are you coming up?"

She responds, "I can't, I have to frost twenty-four more cookies!"

Now he's thinking, *Forget the cookies; come in here and be with me.*

And that's the difference. Most married couples have different love languages, and the key to understanding a love language is to ask yourself: What does my spouse complain about? If she says, "You know, Myron, you're never here, you're always too busy," then she's likely a quality-time person. But maybe he feels that if he gives her enough gifts she'll be happy.

Probably not. The bottom line is: most couples' love languages are not in sync. They collide.

I'm going to be vulnerable for just a moment and share with you that my love language is touch. If you want to love me, touch me. My other language is quality time. I love to have time with my wife. As much as I love our five kids, I kidnap my wife once in a while and take her away for a weekend.

> Write down your top two love languages. (Note: If you have difficulty discerning your primary language, look for clues in what you complain about. A wife's complaint about lack of help around the house, for example, probably means that acts of service is one of her primary love languages.)

DO YOU SPEAK MY LANGUAGE?

Hers:

#1 Love language:

#2 Love language:

Practical Actions:

His:

#1 Love language:

#2 Love language:

Practical Actions:

> Now, as a couple, take turns focusing on that primary love language you've named. Ladies first. Brainstorm a list of ten practical actions that would "speak" to your spouse in this language that he or she loves to hear. Commit to doing many of these things in the months ahead.

Projects for Husbands

Men, what can you do to enhance your marriage relationship? What things will say "I love you" to her? Here are a few general ideas. But it's up to you to turn them into specific acts of love.

Be interested. Find out what your wife enjoys and learn to enjoy it yourself. Or at least learn to enjoy seeing *her* enjoy it. My wife, Sande, is a great "antiquer." So I used to take her to antique shows and wait in the car while she browsed. Somewhere in the process, I started going into the shows and shops with her. I got interested. Now I like all those old tables and chairs and mirrors and porcelains as much as she does.

Become a better listener. If you have little kids, your wife especially needs good conversation (away from them). You're the one to provide it, but it demands excellent listening skills.

You've probably heard this statement before: "I know you believe you understand what you think I said, but I'm not sure you are aware that what you heard is not what I meant." What a challenge to hear something like that and try to do something about it in a marriage! It takes a solid commitment of time, concentration, and patience to untangle our misperceptions, to confront our penchant for "talking past" one another. It's hard to keep checking to make sure we actually hear what's being said. That's because being attentive is harder than making snap judgments and immediate assumptions. Talking and listening is more difficult than just clamming up. Clarifying our needs is tougher than merely announcing our demands a little louder.

Consider the marital situations below. As a good listener, can you tell what's really being said? Write a statement in the blank spaces telling what you think the speaker means.

When you're through, check the end of this session to find out the actual meanings in the minds of the speakers. Then, as a whole group, compare and discuss what you thought the speaker was saying with the actual meaning intended.

Optional: Also discuss these questions: How common are misunderstandings like these in a marriage? How can we be more direct in our speech with our spouses?

---

1. Juanita walks up to Ricardo as he sits in the living-room chair on a beautiful Saturday morning. She looks out the window for a moment and says, "Oh, you're reading the paper *now?*"

   - What she's really saying:

2. Todd unleashes a huge, toothy smile and says to his wife, "You really seemed to enjoy Jack's company tonight."

   ▪ What he's really saying:

3. Jennifer comes home to find her husband at the ironing board. She says, "I notice you're using a lot of starch on my shirts lately."

   ▪ What she's really saying:

4. Jason is falling asleep after sex, feeling warm and relaxed. His wife, Jane, turns to him and says, "Do you think we could take a vacation soon—just the two of us?"

   ▪ What she's really saying:

5. The snow is falling outside as Bill sits at the kitchen table surveying the stack of bills in front of him. He looks up at Betty and says heatedly, "I can't believe you spent $100 on new coats for the kids!"

   ▪ What he's really saying:

Be focused on enjoyment. King Solomon, the writer of Ecclesiastes, puts it this way:

> *Enjoy life with your wife, whom you love,*
> *all the days of this meaningless life*
> *that God has given you under the sun—*
> *all your meaningless days.* (Ecclesiastes 9:9)

Meaningless life translates as "mist of mists." Holding on to life is like trying to hold on to something that's drifting by. We need to go ahead and enjoy it, rather than store up pleasure for another time.

Be a gentle maestro. Are you acquainted with the late Arthur Fiedler, the great conductor? We men are the Arthur Fiedlers of our marriage. We can gracefully, gently, and elegantly coax the music out of this relationship. We may have to learn gentleness by trial and error, discovering what says "I love you" to our wives and then determining to do those things. It will be worth it! For example, we can learn and practice the truth that sex begins in the morning before we head off to work. It starts with taking out the garbage. It starts with putting her needs first. That, not the feminization of men, is tender leadership.

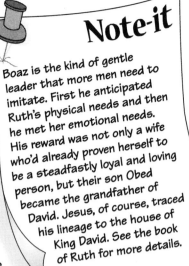

Note-it

Boaz is the kind of gentle leader that more men need to imitate. First he anticipated Ruth's physical needs and then he met her emotional needs. His reward was not only a wife who'd already proven herself to be a steadfastly loyal and loving person, but their son Obed became the grandfather of David. Jesus, of course, traced his lineage to the house of King David. See the book of Ruth for more details.

Form your men's and women's groups once again, read the Scripture verse on the following page, and move through the discussion questions that follow. Then each group will create separate acrostics using the letters in the word "considerate" on a large sheet of paper or poster board. The acrostics should use words or phrases that describe "what a considerate husband is like."

Tape the men's and women's acrostics to the wall and spend some time comparing them. Discuss together: (1) Where did we men and women most agree? and (2) Where did we least agree? Why?

(Note: Don't be afraid to have some fun with this!)

CONSIDERATE HUSBANDS

Husbands, in the same way be considerate as you live with your wives, and treat them with respect as the weaker partner and as heirs with you of the gracious gift of life, so that nothing will hinder your prayers. (1 Peter 3:7)

1. What did Peter first ask for from husbands in his instructions to them regarding their wives?

2. In your own words, define "considerate."

3. What do you think Peter meant by "weaker partner"?

C

O

N

S

I

D

E

R

A

T

E

Priorities for Wives

We've talked about projects for husbands that can enhance the relationship. Now it's time to focus on the things wives can do to keep a marriage humming along. I'm going to suggest three things here, and each builds upon the other.

Be in pursuit. Yes, pursue him relentlessly! Go ahead, call him at work. Just imagine the man who opens his briefcase at work—and then quickly slams it shut on top of his desk. He can't believe what he just saw. He thinks it's a pair of his wife's panties, but he's not quite sure. They're in his briefcase and there's a note on them saying: "The children will be gone and I'm going to get home early. Meet me at the house at four. . . ."

I know it sounds strange to put this kind of advice in a biblical curriculum—but if you do that kind of thing for a man, he becomes a clock watcher all day long! If your upbringing wouldn't let you go that far, put just a little intimate note into his lunch pail, or put a Post-it™ note on his car steering wheel the night before. Rent a day room at a motel and kidnap him. Let him know you've got the hots for him—that you just can't stand to be apart. Are you getting the picture? The Bible makes it clear that in marriage we should be celebrating our union—sexually, intimately—at every opportunity to come together as a couple.

Note-it

Do you know the ABCDs of meeting your spouse's needs? If we were to condense some of the ideas in this session—and make them alphabetical—it would be easier to recall them (and do them) at a moment's notice:

Husbands
Affectionately love her. Remember that good hygiene is important for this.
Become more conversational. Develop an interest in what she's interested in.
Commit to listening to her and spending time with her. Resist the urge to fix things.
Discover her love language. Then lead her gently.

Wives
Assert yourself. A husband loves it when his wife aggressively pursues him.
Be respectful. Let him know you admire his abilities and judgments. And guard the privacy in your relationship.
Creatively please him. Come up with new ideas for the bedroom (and not just related to the decor).
Develop companionship. You are lovers, but you're also best friends, right?

There aren't too many men who don't like the idea of their wives pursuing their chubby little bodies. I thank God that Sande still pursues me once in a while. It's not her style, but she takes the lead sometimes because she knows that's important to me.

Admittedly, that's difficult for many because so many of us had negative experiences and were taught just the opposite in childhood. Yet men are very physical. They bring a physical presence to marriage. That's why when the fourth-grade boy is hitting the girl, we say, "He likes you."

Be aggressive in your pursuit. Initiate sex. Undress him. One year Sande and I were in Toronto when we celebrated our wedding anniversary. So I picked out a restaurant with lots of forks and made a dinner reservation. I got all dressed up. I was shouting at her (yelling is one of my spiritual gifts), doing the husband-gets-impatient routine.

"We're gonna be late!"

She's in the bathroom getting ready.

She comes out in a negligee.

"I thought we'd eat in," she says.

As if on cue, there's a knock on the door. "Room service."

Sande whisks away, out of sight. I go to the door and open it. I'm so dumbfounded, the waiter has to ask me if he can come in.

He delivers a meal. He leaves.

Sande comes back out. She goes to a drawer, pulls out two candles, and lights them. . . . I'm not going to provide any more details, because I think you get the picture.

Be aggressive, wives. Your husbands will love you for it.

Be creative in your aggressive pursuit. How creative can you be? Consider the case of Karen and Larry. Here was a guy whose marriage felt stale to him, rut-like. He was a blue-collar worker, with three kids and a repairman job at the local auto garage. His wife was brought up in a modest, strict, and controlling home. She believed that sex was something she—*unfortunately*—had to deal with once in a while, and she sort of went through the motions. In the meantime, this marriage was dying—they were fighting and not getting along.

> If sensuality were happiness, beasts would be happier than men; but human felicity is lodged in the soul, not in the flesh.
>
> —Seneca

When I met with Karen, I felt as though I was talking to a little girl instead of a grown woman with three kids; she just didn't understand. So I said, "You know, your husband picked you out of all the women he dated. He picked you. You're it. He said, 'I want to spend the rest of my life with this woman.' So you've really got to understand how he thinks in this area of your marriage."

I then talked with her about sexual fulfillment. She immediately responded with, "But I do have sex with him! I never turn him down for it. When he wants sex, I give him sex."

"Karen," I said, "You're missing the point here. It's not the purely mechanistic act of sex that matters so much; it's the emotional part. Larry needs to know that you want him. Really want him. He wants to feel that he needs him, and when you don't convey that, you emasculate him. You've cut him to the quick."

Then I gave her the basics. I asked her, "Do you want to respect your husband?"

"Oh, of course I do." (After all, this was a woman who grew up with the importance of respect—that was her middle name.)

"If you want to respect your husband, you're going to make him feel that he's wanted. That's how you respect this relationship." I read aloud 1 Corinthians 7:3-5 and asked what it meant to her. Her response: "Paul says, 'Do it.'"

You should have seen her as I paraphrased the passage: "If you want to stop for prayer, you can do that, but go back and do it again."

I had her laughing at that point. She thought it was funny. But I wanted her to see that when she has no expectations for the sexual side of marriage, she is turning her man off, giving him no motivation to do anything either. Then the woman becomes merely a sexual receptacle, a dumping ground. And that doesn't feel good for anybody.

So I walked her through these ideas and then summarized, "There's this little boy inside your husband who really needs to feel needed, and one of the ways that men need to feel needed is in the sexual sense. I mean, your husband is in his late thirties, he's starting to be follicly challenged, and he's put on a few pounds. But when you come on to him, when you become assertive, you've got that little boy in him just jumping up and down."

I'm sorry to be so blunt about all of this, but I know Karen benefited from this heart-to-heart conversation. And the next time I saw Larry he blurted, "Hey, Doc, I don't know what you said to my wife, but it worked great!"

Keep in mind that the world paints us men as "emotional nothings" who think through our zippers. Yet we've seen that the most important need for men is sexual fulfillment, not just the physical act. Therefore, women need to be sold on the idea that *they are the ones who dictate the sexual fulfillment* in a marriage, based on their interest in sex, their creativity in sex, and their just flat-out aggressiveness. Clearly, this goes counter to the way many women think of themselves.

A wife needs to know when to be assertive, when to pursue her husband. Read the passage below and discuss the questions on the following page with your spouse.

All night long on my bed I looked for the one my heart loves; I looked for him but did not find him.

I will get up now and go about the city, through its streets and squares; I will search for the one my heart loves. So I looked for him but did not find him.

The watchmen found me as they made their rounds in the city. "Have you seen the one my heart loves?"

Scarcely had I passed them when I found the one my heart loves. I held him and would not let him go till I had brought him to my mother's house, to the room of the one who conceived me. (Song of Songs 3:1-3)

- Who is the pursuer here? Male or female?

- Wives, ask your husband if he would enjoy this kind of pursuit.

- Husbands, what could you suggest as a good way for your wife to pursue you in the days ahead?

 To close your session, talk about your joys and concerns over the past week. Then assign specific requests to people before bowing for a time of prayer.

Keeping the Promise

1. Husbands, give extra hugs this week. Keep in mind that your goal is not sex.

2. Wives, try joining your husband in an activity he enjoys. Make sure it's one that you *don't* enjoy! Be his recreational helpmate.

3. As a couple, resolve not to split up at the next party or event that you attend together.

4. Wives, plan a romantic evening this week for your spouse. It doesn't have to be an expensive night out, but unearth the candles, turn on the soft music . . . (you get the idea).

5. Try this "He Said / She Said" discussion starter: Historically and culturally, society has portioned out roles to men and women in marriage. How do those roles match up with what you know of "her needs" and "his needs" in marriage?

Commitment Check

Couples of Promise commit themselves to making time for each other. Have you planned a regular date night or romantic getaway into your calendars? Take the time to do that now.

> **Answers to the "What are they really saying?" exercise on pages 105-106:**
> 1. "I sure wish you'd mow the lawn."
> 2. "Man, am I *jealous!*"
> 3. "I love nice, starched shirts for my work uniform. I can't believe how blessed I am! My husband irons for me! I sure want this guy to know how much I'm in love with him."
> 4. "I'm not feeling very close to you these days. We need time to talk."
> 5. "Looks like I'm just not making the grade as a provider. Either I get a raise, or I'm finding a night job!"

For further information, consider:

Leman, Kevin. *What a Difference a Daddy Makes*, Nashville, Tenn.: Nelson, 1999.

Leman, Kevin. *Women Who Try Too Hard: Breaking the Pleaser Habits*. Grand Rapids, Mich.: Revell, 1997.

Wakefield, Norman. *Listening, A Christian's Guide to Loving Relationship*. Dallas, Tex.: Word, 1981.

NOTES

1. James B. Nelson, *The Intimate Connection* (Philadelphia, Penn.: Westminster Press, 1988).
2. Adapted from Keven Leman, *Keeping Your Family Together When the World Is Falling Apart* (Colorado Springs, Colo.: Focus on the Family, 1993), p. 139.
3. See Gary Chapman, *The Five Love Languages* (Chicago: Northfield Publishing, 1992), chapters 4–8.

Affairproof Your Marriage!

S arah woke up in a daze. The twins were screaming again, needing to be fed and then changed. It was like clockwork with those two. Of course, Ted was already gone for the day and wouldn't be back until midnight.

Another round of drudgery, crying babies, and searing loneliness.

The one bright spot was her part-time job, Wednesdays and Fridays at the radio station. Sarah could leave the twins at her mother's and spend a few glorious hours doing what she loved—playing favorite tunes for the fans of her afternoon call-in show.

Her manager, Ron, was especially friendly and appreciated her talent. He also seemed to understand her growing frustrations at home. Ron had even mentioned that he and his wife, Cindy, weren't getting along very well, so he could definitely relate. After a couple hours of working and talking with Ron, Sarah always felt happier, as if she'd had a huge weight lifted off her shoulders.

She knew it was probably dangerous in some way, but her thoughts were focusing more on Ron than on Ted in the past few weeks.

Danger . . . or excitement?

In any case, engineering school was consuming her husband, and all the late hours at the lab and library were turning him into a stranger at home. He said it would only be for another year. But could she hold out?

For now, it was enough to think about Ron's sweet, gentle eyes. . . .

As a supplement to this session, view "How to Affairproof Your Marriage" on the videotape "Keeping the Promise," Tape 2. If you wish, launch this session by playing the opening skit on this section of the tape.

Keep Satisfaction High

You may not know a Sarah and Ted or a Ron and Cindy. But you probably recognize the kinds of problems and temptations they're facing. Actually, the names aren't important because the issues involved are virtually universal. It's the story of a husband and wife gradually growing apart, subtly being pulled into the swirling waters that lead to an affair. If it hasn't happened to you, rejoice! But be aware: the possibility is always lurking.

> It takes two to make a marriage a success and only one to make it a failure.
> —Herbert Samuel

How can we avoid getting anywhere near that murky river whose seemingly gentle current will eventually send us plummeting over the precipice? The first thing to know about marital affairs is this: *satisfied partners don't wander.*

That's right: affairproofing a marriage is all about meeting one another's needs. Over the years, in dealing with hundreds of people, I've discovered a one-to-one relationship between what went on in the affair and what was lacking in the marriage. Persons who have succumbed to the temptation of an affair often say to me in counseling, "You're not gonna believe this, but . . . "

When they say "but," I interrupt. "Let me tell you. Sex didn't start this thing."

Affairs Start with Need

Those who say, "That could never happen to me," are the ones I worry about the most. The Bible makes it clear that temptation will always be there, but the disillusionment stage of marriage is when you're most vulnerable to an affair. It happens in one of those weak moments. You're not feeling affirmed by your spouse, and someone comes up to you at the water cooler at work and says, "I love that outfit." Or "I like that tie." You're so starved for attention or a little kindness; you find yourself thinking about that person later in the day. You wonder if you'll see him or her again. The point is, people rarely start off with, "Gee, I think I'd like to have sex with him." No, they start with a much deeper need.

One guy, an elder in his church, called me and said, "My wife and I are having communication problems. Will you see us?"

We had three sessions. But after three sessions with this couple, I still didn't have the foggiest idea why we were meeting. I had, however, violated my own counseling rules. Usually I see a couple together and then I see them individually. Next I see them together again. Not until the fourth session, however, did I begin individual meetings, first seeing the wife on her own.

When people drop a bomb on you in therapy, they tend to do it right at the end of the hour. Toward the end of our session, she dropped the bomb. "Do you think it would help if I told the truth?"

I said, "Well, we could try it for a while and see how it works."

She confessed to an affair.

I didn't suspect. In fact, she'd had three affairs under super-Christian's nose. This is the guy who almost every night of the week was out in the name of Christ doing God's work. He was at every church meeting. He was at meetings he didn't have to be at. He was that kind of a guy. If there was a workday at church that started at 9 A.M., he'd be there at 8:30 with shovel in hand.

> Lord, make me chaste—but not yet.
>
> —St. Augustine

I don't want to excuse this woman's affairs, but if the man had his priorities in line and was the kind of husband he needed to be to his wife, she would never have looked for someone else. And sadly for her, the church was the enemy. Remember: *affairs are the tragic result of unmet needs within a marriage.*

What's your SQ*?
Think about your relationship with your spouse these days. What is your level of satisfaction in the marriage?

Husbands, mark an "H" where you are on each scale on the following page; wives, mark a "W." When you're both through marking the satisfaction scales, take some time to share your responses (preferably at home, with no limits on the time!). Be sure to follow these rules:

1. Take turns speaking, and then listening, as you deal with the six areas.
2. When speaking, use "I" statements only—make no accusations of any kind.
3. When listening, hear your spouse out until he or she is through talking about an area—listen without interrupting, seeking only to gather information and to hear your spouse's heart.
4. Have no other agenda or plans at this time, other than to communicate as clearly as possible and to listen as deeply as you can.

*Satisfaction Quotient

1. When it comes to receiving encouragement and support from my spouse, I . . .

1	**2**	**3**	**4**	**5**
"Can't get no satisfaction"				"Couldn't be more satisfied"

2. When it comes to *feeling* needed, wanted, and loved, I . . .

1	**2**	**3**	**4**	**5**
"Can't get no satisfaction"				"Couldn't be more satisfied"

3. When it comes to communication in this marriage, I . . .

1	**2**	**3**	**4**	**5**
"Can't get no satisfaction"				"Couldn't be more satisfied"

4. When it comes to having a spouse who understands my deepest needs and most precious goals and dreams, I . . .

1	**2**	**3**	**4**	**5**
"Can't get no satisfaction"				"Couldn't be more satisfied"

5. When it comes to sexual fulfillment, I . . .

1	**2**	**3**	**4**	**5**
"Can't get no satisfaction"				"Couldn't be more satisfied"

6. When it comes to (fill in the blank) _____, I . . .

1	**2**	**3**	**4**	**5**
"Can't get no satisfaction"				"Couldn't be more satisfied"

Note-it

According to a recent confidential survey, 37 percent of pastors admitted to being inappropriately involved with a church member. (Also, seventy percent of pastors indicated that they did not have what they considered a close friend or accountability partner.) Do you see a connection here?

Affairs Can Be Avoided

The good news, of course, is that an affair is never inevitable. Every one of them could have been avoided. Here are some of the ways we can ensure ourselves against their devastating effects.

Pledge your commitment. What has happened to the idea of commitment in our society? Just consider the numbers of young people choosing to live together today. They probably think it's best to "test drive" a relationship before buying into it for good. Research suggests, however, that there's actually a higher divorce rate for those who've lived together first! You see, living together is still merely dating in its heaviest form. The masks still don't come off. And you can't gauge the strength of a relationship until the masks come off—which requires the forever-after commitment of marriage vows.

My former colleague, Randy Carlson, once went to his kids, aged seventeen, fourteen, and ten, and told them, "Your mother and I will never divorce. That's our pledge to you."

How many dads do you know today who stand up before their kids, bring them together at the dinner table and say, "Hey, I want to tell you something: I'm completely committed to this marriage for the rest of my life"? You're walking the plank when you say this; no turning back. Can you hear the water below you?

> Women need a reason to have sex. Men just need a place.
> —from the movie City Slickers

My hat's off to Randy. His story puts in stark contrast the lack of commitment we find in so many "relationships" today. We're living in a Pampers-like society. You know, the Pampers™ gets soiled, you throw it away. The guy isn't perfect, you dump the chump. She's not everything I thought she was—see ya! It's so refreshing, then, to hear someone say, "You know, it was my fault." It's refreshing to hear people say, "Forgive me, I was wrong." This is what people in marriage need to model. We must balance responsibility with for-giveness and love. And all of this flows from a lifetime commitment.

Treat one another as persons, not things. This isn't as easy as it may sound, especially for men. I think many of us men view women in a certain way. I call it the gold coin theory. We see women as valuable. Like a gold coin you stick in your pocket, you put her away. Then you pull her out when needed.

We need to treat all people as persons—even our spouses! None of us wants to feel used in a marriage, no matter how wonderful our husband or wife may be in every other area. For example, I talk to a lot of pastors and I tell them to give their spouses free rein. These pastors are reaching out to hundreds of people every year, showing great care and empathy and compassion. But they can lose sight of the per-son by their side. They can begin to see that spouse merely as a fellow worker in the ministry, rather than as a person to be cherished and loved in the marriage. So I tell pastors not to collar a spouse with certain "expected" functions and respon-sibilities in the church. He or she has primary responsibilities to the family and to the children. After that, when it comes to the ministry involvement, it's up for grabs.

How do you view your spouse—mostly as a person or as a thing? Be careful, this can be subtle!

Among the choices on the following page, choose the top three ways you tend to view your spouse. Mark a 1 next to your top choice and 2 and 3 next to the second and third choices. (If none of the listed views seems to fit, write your own next to "other.") When you're through, compare responses with your spouse and explain *the reasons* for your choices. Then discuss the question that follows.

Husbands:
In general, I tend to view my wife as . . . (mark 1, 2, 3)

___ a trophy on a pedestal
___ a domestic employee
___ a second mom
___ a fun buddy
___ a little girl
___ a work partner
___ a romantic lover
___ a demanding taskmaster
___ a best friend
___ an enchanting princess
___ other:

___ other:

___ other:

Wives:
In general, I tend to view my husband as . . . (mark 1, 2, 3)

___ a trophy
___ a knight in shining armor
___ a romantic lover
___ a demanding taskmaster
___ a best friend
___ a savior
___ a workhorse and paycheck
___ a fun date
___ a second daddy
___ a big brother
___ other:

___ other:

___ other:

Both:
How would you *like* to be viewed in your spouse's eyes? Why?

Put spouse and family first. If you want to do yourself a favor and protect your marriage from an affair, you'll put your spouse first. That's anti-American, of course. What most of us are actually hearing in society is "I've got to be me." That means everything *but* the marriage must come first, especially the career. But marriage is like a plant. It must be watered and nurtured regularly. If you don't care for it, it withers.

Read the following verse from the Bible's famous "love chapter":

Love is patient, love is kind. It does not envy, it does not boast, it is not proud. It is not rude, it is not self-seeking, it is not easily angered, it keeps no record of wrongs. (1 Corinthians 13:4-5)

Note-it

A word to the men: You know that sexual temptation is a tough daily problem. Here are some notes that may help as you continue to find ways to "walk away" from enticement:

- Often, we just don't realize we're under attack until it's too late. Think about the constant bombardment of sexual images that come through in the media these days. Can you admit that it's a problem?
- Have you ever heard (or said): "The day I stop looking is the day I die" or "Just because I'm married doesn't mean I can't window shop"? This is lust, gentlemen. And it feeds temptation!
- I've often heard that it all started "innocently," with no physical contact. But remember: Mental affairs can be as destructive as physical affairs. This is usually a surprise attack, not a premeditated act. Be ready to run!
- We have forgotten *who* we are and *whose* we are. Take a moment to read Ephesians 1:3-14 and Revelation 1:12-18, 4:1-11. You've been saved by an awesome Savior! Your identity: a beloved son. Live like it!
- Have you taken up the "spiritual tools of victory"? Here they are: gratitude, surrender to God's will, reliance on the Holy Spirit's help, prayer, spiritual fruit (see Galatians 5:16-26), and the full armor of God (see Ephesians 6:10-20).
    - Men tend to be loners. Because we're usually trying to battle alone, the lack of accountability pulls us under. So find a small group in which you can share your deepest needs and fears. Stay in contact with regular "progress reports"!

It's clear that love doesn't demand its own way but is essentially giving. To adhere to that standard, we've got to make the tough decisions for the good of our spouse and family. How does that look in real life? For me, it means turning down lots of speaking engagements every year. I recall talking over the phone with a man in Hershey, Pennsylvania, who wanted me to come and speak, but I turned him down. The date he had in mind was my daughter's birthday. The man called back, saying, "We have worked it out for your daughter to come with you."

He didn't get it. "This is a family celebration," I told him. "And I can't come."

He missed the point: *The whole is more important than the parts.* My family was more important than a part of my schedule. Her birthday was more important than another of my speaking engagements. And the thing is, our kids are always taking mental notes. Even our decisions about the little things make a great impact on them.

Part of the problem is that sometimes the kids will even tell you, "I don't want you there." When my daughter Krissy had her first high-school volleyball game, she made it clear to me and her mother that she didn't want us there. (Her mother gets too excited and yells too much; I always remain perfectly calm and serene.) So I drove her to the game, conveniently located sixty-five miles from our home, and dropped her off.

Later, when I walk into the gym, Krissy, age fifteen, is in set position, ready to play volleyball. She waves to me—just a couple of fingers twitching briefly in my direction.

And what does that little wave mean? "Hi, Dad! Glad you're here."

Making such events a priority in your life will meet deep needs in your family members. The number-one priority has to be your spouse, and then the children.

Keep deepening the intimacy. We need to make sure that our marriages are everything they can be in terms of intimacy. Remember what I said, marriage isn't just a 50/50 proposition; it is a 100/100 commitment. When we give of ourselves completely, holding nothing back, we make ourselves transparent and vulnerable. That's taking a great risk. But it's the only way to deepen the intimacy.

Think about this. Remember how much effort you put into the relationship when you were dating? You took a shower before the date, did your hair, bought a new outfit. Everything was designed to put your best foot forward.

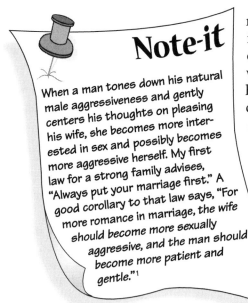

When a man tones down his natural male aggressiveness and gently centers his thoughts on pleasing his wife, she becomes more interested in sex and possibly becomes more aggressive herself. My first law for a strong family advises, "Always put your marriage first." A good corollary to that law says, "For more romance in marriage, the wife should become more sexually aggressive, and the man should become more patient and gentle."[1]

The same kind of effort is required *after* marriage, when it comes to deepening the intimacy. It's hard work, but intimacy will deepen. Or it will die of sheer neglect. So, what have you done this week to affirm your husband or wife? Do you "date" your spouse often? Do you set aside special time for yourselves as a couple, just to talk? The point is this: *If you don't have an ongoing love affair with your spouse, there's a high probability that someone else will!*

It's a sad thing to say, but you can buy just about everything that's included in a marriage. You can buy companionship; you can buy sex. But you can't buy intimacy. You can buy a housekeeper, someone to cook your meals, someone to mow the lawn.

But you can't buy intimacy.

Have you considered the practical difference between a 50/50 approach to your marriage and a 100/100 approach? How do they look in a real marriage, and how does the 100/100 approach tend to deepen intimacy?

Form three groups or pairs, each focusing on one of the following scenarios. First discuss the differences between 50/50 and 100/100, in general. Then develop a set of actions for the husband and the wife in the scenario; describe the things they would probably do in each case. Finally, come back together as a whole group to talk about your responses.

Sally has been working as Howard's assistant for five years. They get along wonderfully and seem to have a friendship that goes beyond just the employee-employer relationship. But Sally's husband, Bill, has been wondering lately if Sally and Howard are becoming "too friendly." Once again Sally has stayed late at the office. Tonight, as soon as she arrives home, she announces, "Howard is being moved to the new building on the other side of town. He wants me to move there with him. I'll even get a promotion, a raise, and a brand new office with a beautiful view overlooking the river! What do you think, Bill?"

50/50 RESPONSE
What the HUSBAND does:

100/100 RESPONSE
What the HUSBAND does:

What the WIFE does:

What the WIFE does:

Newlywed Phyllis just wishes she had more time with Oscar during the week. They're both working so hard, putting in such long hours. Oscar even has a night job. One evening, while putting some of Oscar's clothes away, Phyllis comes across some pornography hidden away at the back of a bottom drawer. She's still in a state of shock when Oscar walks in, all smiles. He says with a wink, "I got off early tonight! Want to *you know?*"

50/50 RESPONSE

What the HUSBAND does:

100/100 RESPONSE

What the HUSBAND does:

What the WIFE does:

What the WIFE does:

Roger's father—his "best friend"—died suddenly three months ago. Even with all the weeks that have passed, Jill has noticed that Roger doesn't seem to be pulling out of his grief and depression. He sits around a lot, looking out the window, mostly mumbling responses when Jill tries to start a conversation. When Roger does talk it's usually over the phone to Shirley, the neighbor across the street. In fact, Roger spends hours talking to Shirley, and it does brighten his mood. Tonight, as Roger heads for the phone, Jill says, "Since you're going to be busy again all evening, I'm going out for a while. . . . Want to know where I'm going?"

50/50 RESPONSE

What the HUSBAND does:

100/100 RESPONSE

What the HUSBAND does:

What the WIFE does:

What the WIFE does:

Discuss as a whole group: What things are required of spouses in order to move from 50/50 toward 100/100 in their marriages?

Note-it

More thoughts on having victory over sexual temptation:

- Understand that sex is beautiful only in the marriage container (see Song of Songs 8:6-7). Direct all your sexual focus on your spouse in love-service.
- Differentiate between temptation and sin. Remember that even Jesus was tempted in every way — but remained sinless. Therefore, end the self-condemnation. You are not disqualified!
- When tempted to roam, recognize that you're in a very real battle. Get righteously angry. See the manipulation. Fight back!
- If you fail, understand the complete forgiveness that Jesus gives you. This stimulates gratitude, which leads to obedience.
- Stop feeding the temptation — right now (see Job 31:1). Then remove the potential temptations around you. (In other words, it's time to analyze the availability of cable TV sex, movie sex, Internet sex, and so on. Take action!)
- Fight discouragement when you fail. Remember that growth sometimes means two steps forward and one step back. Envision your life as a large cup of cold water into which falls the occasional drop of ink. You can't fight against the ink, or even remove it. But you can keep adding water (doing the right thing), more and more, year after year. That is the way to purify your life!

Keep Temptation Low

We've seen that the key to affairproofing is keeping the satisfaction levels as high as possible. This requires a 100 percent commitment to our spouse's highest good. But there's another side to this fight for a faithful marriage, as if we were waging war on two fronts. While we're building love and goodwill on the satisfaction front, we've got to keep attacking the temptation front. That battle never ceases, does it?

Flee the Allurement (Don't Wander)

The Bible makes it clear: there will always be temptation. Just when we're so thankful that everything is going great. Just when we've apparently reached a new level of victory over loneliness or lust or frustration. And especially when we're perfectly confident in our willpower to resist. Just then, we're set up for a fall. So the question is: how do we stay on our feet and keep moving ahead?

The answer: *Run!*

 In a few minutes of silence, meditate upon the Bible passages below. Then mark the sentences and phrases as suggested. When you're through, divide into small groups to talk about your markings and to discuss the questions at the end of this exercise.

- UNDERLINE the sentence or phrase that speaks to you most powerfully and directly in your current situation.
- CIRCLE a sentence or phrase that leads you to offer thanks and praise to God.
- Draw a QUESTION MARK next to any sentences or phrases that raise questions or concerns in your mind.
- Draw a STAR next to a sentence or phrase that makes you want to pray about your need.
- Jot an EXCLAMATION POINT next to sentences or phrases that inspire you to grow and mature in your struggles with temptation.

After a while his master's wife took notice of Joseph and said, "Come to bed with me!" But he refused. "With me in charge," he told her, "my master does not concern himself with anything in the house; everything he owns he has entrusted to my care. No one is greater in this house than I am. My master has withheld nothing from me except you, because you are his wife. How then could I do such a wicked thing and sin against God?" And though she spoke to Joseph day after day, he refused to go to bed with her or even be with her.

One day he went into the house to attend to his duties, and none of the household servants was inside. She caught him by his cloak and said, "Come to bed with me!" But he left his cloak in her hand and ran out of the house. (Genesis 39:7-12)

Blessed is the man who does not walk in the counsel of the wicked or stand in the way of sinners or sit in the seat of mockers. (Psalm 1:1)

Flee from sexual immorality. All other sins a man commits are outside his body, but he who sins sexually sins against his own body. (1 Corinthians 6:18)

No temptation has seized you except what is common to man. And God is faithful; he will not let you be tempted beyond what you can bear. But when you are tempted, he will also provide a way out so that you can stand up under it. (1 Corinthians 10:13)

Abstain from all appearance of evil. (1 Thessalonians 5:22, KJV)

Consider it pure joy, my brothers, whenever you face trials of many kinds, because you know that the testing of your faith develops perseverance. Perseverance must finish its work so that you may be mature and complete, not lacking anything. . . .

Blessed is the man who perseveres under trial, because when he has stood the test, he will receive the crown of life that God has promised to those who love him. (James 1:2-4,12)

Note-it

King David did a lot of things right in his life, but he will be remembered as much for what he did wrong. He committed the sin of adultery with Bathsheba, who also was married at the time. They stayed a couple, but at great cost—the murder of her husband Uriah and the loss of their firstborn son, who died as a consequence of their sin.

1. What practical actions are suggested in these passages to keep us from wandering?

2. Why do you think sexual sin is a sin against oneself?

3. Recall Joseph and his encounters with Potiphar's wife. What is the difference between wandering and fleeing? Do you believe Joseph was rewarded or penalized for his courage?

4. What things have helped you to "flee" in the past? What advice about this can you offer to others in your group?

If you think about it, the words *flee* and *wander* are virtually opposites. To wander means to get off track by moving slowly and aimlessly. To flee, on the other hand, suggests moving swiftly away from danger and toward a target. Don't allow yourself into situations where you're going to be overpowered by temptation. In other words, if you're a tricycle person, stay out of the fast lane of life. Know what your limits are.

Fill the Account (Don't Withdraw)

In his book *His Needs, Her Needs,* Willard F. Harley, Jr., talks about what he calls the love bank.[2] Everybody has a love bank, and your spouse's bank is always open. Your job is to make sure you're making deposits every day.

"Gee, you look nice." That's a deposit.

"Honey, I appreciate your making time to go to Karen's volleyball game. It meant a lot to her, too." That's a deposit.

Then there's the cheap shot, when we make a withdrawal: "Oh, you're gonna be that late? You won't be at Bobby's soccer game? Well, all right, you go ahead." That's a subtle withdrawal from the love bank.

We know what our mates need us to do. And all through our married lives, with each encounter, each new decision, each opportunity to relate, we face this tough decision: *fill or withdraw?*

A BAKER'S DOZEN WAYS TO FILL "HIS" LOVE BANK[3]

1. Admire his achievements. Let him know you understand the stress he's under at work. (Obviously, we can flip this around because sixty percent of women work.)
2. Keep your "honey-do" list short and to a reasonable number of items.
3. Don't second-guess him in front of the kids. Disagree in private instead of battling in front of the children.
4. Ask him how you can be more sexually aggressive.
5. Handle his male ego with care. Some of you women are thinking, "Grow up. You men are like little kids." That's right. We're exactly like little kids. Don't you get it? That's the point. We love our little toys. They just cost more money.
6. Accept him as he is. Change yourself, not him.
7. Get rid of habits that annoy him.
8. Make it a point to pay special attention to him rather than centering on the children. Remember that your husband must be number one.
9. Thank him for his contributions to the family without adding, "I only wish . . ."
10. Pray for him.
11. If you've got something for him to read, don't bug him about it. Women are always reading something that people like me write. It'll get read. Asterisk or highlight what you want him to notice.
12. Kidnap him. Take him away for the weekend.
13. If your husband is a Howard the Turtle type, very comfortable under his shell, and you get your psychological pitchfork out, saying, "Come on, out, out, out, out!" Howard's gonna pull his little legs in. Try not asking him any questions for a week. (Likewise, if you have a Howard the Turtle kid, a late bloomer, be patient. A watched bloomer never blooms. Back off. They'll live up to their potential.)

A Baker's Dozen Ways to Fill "Her" Love Bank

1. Treat her as supremely important. Ask her what she thinks. Let her know that you want to know how she feels.
2. Give her frequent hugs, especially if she is down or depressed. Just hold her without lectures or advice.
3. Call if you're going to be late.
4. Always handle her with care in every way.
5. Accept her as she is. Change yourself, not her.
6. Get rid of habits that annoy her.
7. When you help around the house, don't expect a twenty-one-gun salute. I'm famous for this. My wife leaves the coffee cups that I bring her in the morning on her bedside table. My job is to pick them up. So when I do, I clang them together. (Wrong!)
8. Let her know how proud you are that she's your wife. I love to tell Sande that. I'm always proud to have her with me.
9. Pray for her (she should be number one). Pray for her every day. Urgent things should increase your prayer life.
10. Besides remembering birthdays and anniversaries, bring home a gift every now and then—just because you love her.
11. When she shares a problem, don't transform yourself into the Great Fixer. Just listen to her. You don't have to jump in with a solution.
12. You may never understand, but ask for her opinion. Don't surprise her with arbitrary decisions.
13. Never give her a toaster on any special occasion, not even a four-slicer. Ditto for can openers.

After you've had a chance to read through the preceding lists, ask yourself the following questions. Then share your answers with your spouse.

- Which of the Bakers Dozen items would make the largest deposit in your love bank?

- Which would make the largest deposit in your spouse's love bank?

Go back through the lists and choose three of the ways to fill your spouse's love bank. Change each of those three items from a "deposit" into a "withdrawal" by varying—in some small way—what is said or done. Put a frowning face in front of one of these "deposit rewrites" that you've been guilty of doing in your marriage. Determine to talk with your spouse about this in the week ahead. Ask for forgiveness, if necessary.

- Deposit Item #___ becomes a *withdrawal* when . . .

- Deposit Item #___ becomes a *withdrawal* when . . .

- Deposit Item #___ becomes a *withdrawal* when . . .

Sing a prayer of praise! To close your session, sing the doxology or a few praise choruses together. If you're aware that someone in the group plays the guitar or piano, plan in advance for musical accompaniment.

Keeping the Promise

1. Think of some of the things you do regularly—things that make withdrawals from your spouse's love bank. On a separate sheet of paper, why not write a letter asking for forgiveness?

2. Memorize 1 Corinthians 6:18. Recite this passage daily to your spouse. If he or she is completing this study with you, have him or her recite it to you. Check each other's accuracy.

3. Keep a prayer journal on behalf of your spouse. Write down one specific prayer request daily. If you and your spouse don't do so already, consider praying together, as well. Be sure to say aloud the request you've already written down.

4. Review your regular, daily schedules with your spouse. Make note of areas in your schedules that could become periods of vulnerability to temptation. Think of changes you can make to protect yourselves.

5. Try this "He Said / She Said" discussion starter: In what ways have we as Christians failed to protect the biblical concept of monogamy and fidelity?

Commitment Check

Couples of Promise commit themselves to honor God through their thoughts, words, and actions. Pray and ask God to reveal to you any ways that you've failed to honor Him or your spouse, especially in thought.

For further information, consider:

Allendar, Dan. *The Wounded Heart.* Colorado Springs, Colo.: NavPress, 1990.

Ferguson, David, Teresa Ferguson, Chris Thurman, and Holly Thurman. *The Pursuit of Intimacy.* Nashville, Tenn.: Nelson, 1993.

NOTES
1. Adapted from Kevin Leman, *Keeping Your Family Together When the World Is Falling Apart* (Colorado Springs, Colo.: Focus on the Family, 1993), pp. 153-154.
2. Willard F. Harley, Jr., *His Needs, Her Needs* (Old Tappan, NJ: Revell, 1986).
3. Adapted from Leman, *Keeping Your Family Together . . .*

A Marriage That's Great for Your Kids

When Holly was preparing to go away to college for the first time, I teased her mom about it unmercifully. "Pretty soon you're going to say good-bye to your firstborn daughter," I would say.

When the time finally came, we drove her down to this little school in Pennsylvania. A big sign reading "Welcome Parents!" greeted us. We drove over to the female dorm. Within sixty seconds, both cars that we'd brought were unloaded by boys in blue button-down shirts. I remember looking at them and wondering if I was going to be meeting one of those boys on a personal basis one day, because they seemed to be checking out the freshmen girls—including my daughter.

We went to all the meetings for parents, and we met lots of people. We met the roommate. We met the parents of the roommate. We were welcomed by far too many people. Clearly it was time for us to go.

"Come on, we need to leave," I said, nudging Sande.

My wife shot a surprised look in my direction. "I haven't made up Holly's bed yet," she said.

"She's in college now," I protested. "She can make her own bed."

Sande, who is a gentle woman, gave me a ferocious look that said, *Back off!* In other words, this bed-making event might be one of her final acts of mothering. She was not to be sidetracked. I backed off.

133

But eventually it really was clear that it was time to go. Holly started saying good-bye to us right on the spot, but I wanted a little more privacy for this special moment, so I asked her to walk us outside. There I watched as mother and daughter hugged each other and said good-bye.

Then Holly hugged me. To my utter surprise, I wouldn't let her go. I broke into tears. As unrelated as it sounds, I stood there, hugging her, thinking about her bra, the one she left on the bathroom floor when she was ten years old. I had picked it up and waved it through the air. I honestly didn't know what it was. So I found Sande and asked, "What is this?"

"That's Holly's bra."

"A bra?" I admit, it did look like something that might grow up and *become* a bra someday. This was what went through my mind as I hugged my firstborn daughter good-bye that day.

"You've got to go," Holly reminded me.

Being a take-charge kind of man, I turned her around to send her on her way. She walked off.

"Call us tonight," I yelled after her.

She didn't look back.

My wife and I looked at each other. We each spent a miserable two and a half hours on our drive home. Holly didn't call. I knew she *shouldn't* call. I was dean of students for eleven years at the University of Arizona, and I knew that she shouldn't call. But I wanted her to call anyway.

Finally, seven days later, Holly called. I ran to the phone when it was my turn to talk to her.

"What were you thinking about when you said good-bye?" I asked her.

"That you and Mom brought me up right. And now it was my time to go into the world myself."

As a supplement to this session, view "A Marriage That's Great for Your Kids" on the videotape "Keeping the Promise," Tape 2. If you wish, launch this session by playing the opening skit on this section of the tape. Then ask your group members, "When it comes to 'clean and neat,' is your personality more like the man's or the woman's in this little mini-drama? Can you share an example?"

Let Them Have Childhood

We do, eventually, have to let go and let our children launch into lives of their own. It's not easy. We've formed strong bonds and we prefer to keep those bonds tight and strong. Instead, we're forced to stretch the relationship, perhaps over long distances and for long periods of time.

But there's an equally irksome difficulty that can plague us parents: the desire to push our kids too quickly into adulthood. When we succumb to this temptation, we rob them of childhood.

Too Pushed and Hurried?

When it comes to raising those little ones, watch out for the tyranny of the urgent. Someone has said: *The urgent is never important; the important is never urgent.*

It's true, isn't it? We all do the urgent things; we don't necessarily do the important things. We may not take time to do the training that our moms and dads did with us when we were kids. We may fail to teach our children early enough in life that "this is right" and "that is wrong." Yet kids need parameters and solid guidance from their earliest days. And much of it flows into them from pure observation. So keep in mind that the kids are always watching, always taking notes.

For some families, switching from the urgent to the important means radical change—like taking the kids out of virtually every activity they're involved in, saving them from drowning in their swirling schedules. In one of my books I titled a chapter, "Help! I'm a Cabby, and My Minivan Isn't Even Yellow!" Can you relate to the cabby mentality in your household? Are you doing nothing but hauling kids around all day, all weekend? It may be time to trade in the family cab for the family living room!

On our television program, "Realfamilies," mom after mom reports spending significant amounts of time taking kids places. If your child is involved in three or four regular weekly activities, and you've got three children, what's your life like? Oprah Winfrey recently did a segment on her talk show all about "families that eat dinner together." This is big news? Apparently, these days it is. Next it will be on the news at eleven.

In our home, we don't answer the phone at dinner. This is the time set aside just for talking with one another. By the way, we also pray around the dinner table. Not just table grace, but unscripted, authentic conversation with God. We love to hear our kids' prayers.

Note-it

If you'd like to do a fuller exploration of the joys and trials of parenting—with practical "how to" advice—order my book *Becoming the Parent God Wants You to Be* (Colorado Springs, Colo: NavPress, 1998). It's a study guide just like this one, for individuals, couples, or groups.

At a glance, would you say your family's lifestyle is too frenetic? In the columns on the following page, jot every activity your family members will participate in this week. But categorize those events according to whether they are merely *urgent* or actually *important* (that is, they contribute to your overall family goals and values).

Optional: Think through the questions that follow this exercise. If possible, discuss them during the week with your spouse and other family members.

THE URGENT AND THE IMPORTANT	
Urgent	**Important**

Go back to the URGENT activities, and answer the following questions.

- Why do these activities seem so pressing?

- What is it about them that keeps them from being in the "important" column?

- How do these activities contribute to, or detract from, your family's priorities, goals, and values?

- What would happen if you decided to do without these activities in your family life?

Go back to the IMPORTANT activities, and answer the following questions.

- What makes these activities so important?

- How are these activities contributing to your family's overall goals and values?

- What would you need to change in your schedules in order to make the important activities a greater priority?

In his book *The Hurried Child*, psychologist David Elkind makes an important point. He says, in essence, that we are hurrying children through their lives. Right after they're born we start looking for the right preschool. We search out the top-notch "academic" institution—Toddler Technical Institute . . . Urchin University . . . Kiddy College. . . . We're hoping to produce what he calls SuperKids. And we assume our SuperKids can handle many pressures, far more than were ever required of us at their age. Sadly, it's a pointless pressure. Yet it's there. And we keep wondering why our kids are so stressed out.[1]

Why not hold back a bit? Grant kids their childhoods. Growing up in my family in western New York state, I didn't have a dime. Every summer, however, we kids made a raft in the creek. Every summer we experienced the same result: It sank. But we created and invented, formed competitions and clubs. And we did it all together.

We played outside. Kids don't play outside now. We prop them up in front of the TV and then wonder why their brains are getting soft. Their sinking ACT scores are a tell-tale sign of this kind of "brain damage."

Sande and I were once faced with the task of getting our nine-year-old daughter across the country. We knew we had the option of putting her on a plane. For an extra fifty dollars the airline would even provide a uniformed person to escort her. Instead, I flew with her across the country and then flew back the same day. In other words, my nine-year-old doesn't fly alone, even if I have to fly five thousand miles in one day.

All I'm saying is this: We push way too many things too early in life on our kids. Kids draw strength from us. If we take things in stride, they take things in stride. But we don't need to push too much on them too soon.

Or Not Challenged Enough?

In some respects, of course, we've pushed too little. Yes, kids need to be kids. But our kids are fatter than ever before; their ACT scores are lower—even on the new, improved, watered-down versions.

Consider the real-life story of Melanie, who hadn't been bringing home any math papers from her private school. Her parents decided to have a conference with the teacher, who said, "Melanie hasn't *elected* math yet." Math is an elective now?

Some schools have even done away with grades. A local news story reported on one school that no longer hands out any Fs. They give Es . . . for "emerging." Your child's emerging, not failing. (I was apparently an emerger when I was in school. My mother used to pray for a C on my report card as a sign there was at least some type of gray matter in my cranial cavity.) So kids don't fail at school. But if you never fail, how do you know when you're succeeding? And how would you learn what it means to seek help and support from others? Clearly, you'd never need it!

Grades for university students have progressively gone up. SAT and ACT scores have been adjusted a couple times to keep from embarrassing our country (any further than it already is) in terms of the intellectual competence of our young people.

We do need to challenge our young people. And as parents we're doing the right thing when we refuse to give our kids a bunch of things. One day my youngest daughter, Lauren, when she was six years old, said to me, "Daddy, is it once-in-a-while today?"

"What do you mean, Honey?"

She repeated it, but with a little more emphasis and a bit of confusion: "Is it once-in-a-while today?"

"Honey, what are you talking about?"

"Once in a while we get a treat, right? Like you said?"

Now I got it. She was talking about that twenty-five-cent treat in a restaurant, the little peppermint patty that comes in a machine. That really made me stop and think. It's so good that she kept my once-in-a-while speech in her heart and waited for that treat until it was the right time. Can you imagine how much better peppermint and chocolate tastes when you save it for "once in a while"? If you give out a peppermint every time you pass the machine, it could get pretty boring. And you've robbed your child of some pure enjoyment.

If we give our kids everything they've ever wanted, if we meet their every emotional need, it's one of the worst things we can do for them. On the other hand, we can build a sense of gratitude in children, and also allow them more happiness in life, as we help them learn how to find the joy in the little things. My point is simple: Find the balance. Let them have their childhoods, but don't fail your children by giving them everything and requiring nothing of them but slipshod effort and half-hearted mediocrity.

There must be a wise and discerning balance between "letting kids be kids" and encouraging a child's best efforts. Mark each case below with an M, L, or B, as suggested. Then, in a small group (1) offer reasons for your choices and (2) tell what you would do as the parent(s) in each case. Be ready for differences of opinion!

M = Pushing too much, too fast
L = Pushing too little, too slow
B = Balanced nicely

___ Eleven-year-old Sharron always liked to sit in her room and draw pictures. She was actually quite good at it, so her parents bought her a professional art-supply kit for her birthday last year. It had everything for drawing—with pencils, paints, or chalk—along with easel, paper, and canvasses. Then they spent weeks looking for a private tutor who began giving her art lessons once a week. Her father also started a file with catalogs from colleges that have excellent art programs.

   When Sharron's parents glanced into her room yesterday, they saw her using the chalk pieces as makeshift curlers for her hair. The easel was in the corner, draped with clothes. Sharron looked up from her desk and said, "Can I go out for the soccer team this year?"

___ As a five-year-old, Heather seemed like a "typical kid" to her parents. The energetic little girl enjoyed being outdoors and having fun with her playmates during the day. In the late afternoons, her parents tended to get involved with things that Heather showed interest in at home, like catching frogs in the back yard, making dandelion bouquets, dancing around like a ballerina with orchestra music, and constructing Lego™ dollhouses. It was usually something different each day, but these activities kept all three of the family members busy.

___ Johnny made straight As throughout elementary school and junior high. In his first semester in high school, he came home with two As, two Bs, and two Cs. His parents were secretly quite disappointed. But they told Johnny, "No problem! We know that high school is a lot more challenging than junior high. And after all, you can never be perfect in life. So don't let it bother you." Johnny said nothing, but walked away with tears forming in his eyes.

___ As a senior, Juan pitched for his 6-A high school baseball team. The team was heading for the state championship, and minor-league scouts were following Juan from game to game, timing his fastballs and paying close attention to his record. Along with loving baseball, Juan was a fine student.

After the semi-final game, a Division I college scout wanted to offer Juan a "full ride" scholarship on the spot. He searched the stands looking for Juan's parents but was told, "They don't usually come to the games." When the scout called Juan's parents at home that evening, they said, "We just want Juan to be happy. We don't believe in putting pressure on him to do anything great with baseball—as long as he's enjoying the game and having fun." After a bit more conversation, the scout promised to call again. But the thought that was running through his mind was: *Those folks sure aren't very cooperative!*

Jot your responses to these two questions about your own childhood and how you approach parenting today. Discuss your answers with your spouse.

---

1. In my family of origin, I was usually . . .

___ pushed too much, too fast.
___ pushed too little, too slow.
___ neither pushed too much, too little.

■ The best example of this is:

2. In our family today, we parents usually . . .

___ push our child(ren) too much, too fast.
___ push too little, too slow.
___ try to keep a balance.

■ The best example of this is:

Let Them See Adulthood

A marriage that's good for your kids is even better for you. Do you believe that as a married couple? In other words, healthy parental relationships now, healthy marriages later. When kids are observing such a relationship over the years, it has a profound impact on them for the good.

Excellent Relating Means So Much to Them

How we couples relate to one another in the family makes such a great impact on kids because . . . *they're always taking notes!* The key relationships in families are father-daughter and mother-son because of the cross-sexual learning going on. As a dad, you not only affirm your daughter's femininity but you also set her up for positive relationships with the opposite sex. As a mom, you influence how your boys will treat their future wives. Let's look at each of these parental roles, in turn, along with the functions of grand-parents and single parents.

The importance of Dad. Norm Wright, in his book *Always Daddy's Girl*, says something quite interesting:

> Like it or not, your father has made a lasting impression on you. Whether he was close or distant, present or absent, cold or warm, loving or abusive, your father has left his mark on you. And your father is still influencing your life today. Probably more than you realize.[2]

Those are truly profound words. We're seeing a movement in our country in which men, husbands and fathers, are taking the initiative and joining groups like Promise Keepers where they can bond with other men. They're standing up and saying, "I want to make a mark in life. I want that mark on my marriage and my family. I'm willing to make some tough choices in life on their behalf."

The importance of Mom. I think when women hear that quote by Norm Wright they probably feel a little slighted, maybe a little jilted. After all, they're the ones who brought these kids into this world, and they have the stretch marks to prove it. They're usually the ones who've been home the most with those little ankle biters, having dealt with them from the time they were twenty inches long until they hit the hormone group. And yet Daddy's presence — or Daddy's absence — can make such a profound difference, especially in his daughter's life.

But it does work the other way, too. As moms raise their boys to be gentlemen — in other words, to put it bluntly, not taking any guff from little Buford — they learn quickly in life that women are to be respected. So guess who they bring home to marry someday? Someone who's similar to you, Mom. That's not so bad, is it?

What I'm saying to you moms, therefore, is that when you hold your son accountable for what he says and does in your relationship, you're actually doing your future daughter-in-law a great service. It makes sense, doesn't it? Mothers have tremendous impact on their sons.

> Form two groups, one consisting of the women in your group and the other consisting of the men. Follow the steps below, jotting your ideas on a large piece of newsprint, if possible. Then report your findings to the whole group.

Men: Study the mother-son relationship of Rebekah and Jacob in Genesis 27:5-17.

Women: Study the father-(step)daughter relationship of Herod and his stepdaughter in Matthew 14:1-12.

- Step 1—List some of the *unhealthy qualities* in this relationship (and in the larger family).

- Step 2—Develop a *modern-day scenario* that has similar dysfunctional dynamics in a parent-child relationship.

- Step 3—Brainstorm *three key guidelines of relating* for father-daughter or mother-son relationships.

The importance of a single parent. In a two-parent home, both spouses play an active role. So it's especially hard for just one parent to hold things together. No one else can fill the missing parent's shoes at home, but sometimes we just have to do the best we can when we're forced to go solo. Women, who so often head the single-parent family, still need to find some masculine input for their children. Often a coach or other community (or church) leader can step in and fill a kid's "guidance void" like no other.

I love the story of Ben Carson, a pediatric neurosurgeon. He grew up in abject poverty with his brother, Curtis, in Detroit. His mother, a devout Christian, was a domestic worker who cleaned houses. This wonderful mother required the boys to do a book report every week. It wasn't until Carson was in junior high that he discovered his mother couldn't read! She knew, however, if there was a way out of the cycle of poverty it was going to be through education. Her lesson to the rest of us: If you're a single parent, be the best single parent you can be.

Now for a special note to those single-parent women who may be feeling hopeless about ever finding help from a good man. I once counseled a woman who had really been burned in life and beaten down. She was a pleaser who chronically acquiesced. She brought men, powerful ones, into her life who used her, but she couldn't see the problem. She'd had an absent father, and it was obvious that she was looking for strength.

"Suppose you met a guy at work who seemed nice and asked you out to dinner. Would you go with him?" I asked her one day. She agreed rather passively that she probably would.

"Suppose he takes you out. You have a great time together. He walks you home, thanks you, then says, 'Could I have the key to your apartment?' You freeze like a rabbit. He says, however, 'I just want to open the door for you.' He opens it, hands back the key, and thanks you.

"You keep talking at work. He asks you out again, to a movie. Would you go? Yeah? You go out again and have a great time again. He says, 'Would you mind if I gave you a kiss good night?' He asks you out again. This time he wants to take your five-year-old daughter with you to the mountains to go camping. Would you go?"

"Oh, yes!"

Notice the difference in the woman's response by this time. Notice what she wants to know now. Where is this man coming from? That's what she wants to know. This is a woman who's been sexually active since age thirteen, used and abused by every man she knows. She just wants to be loved. That's what she really wants in life.

The good news for women is there are men like that in this world. There are men who love their God, think enough of Him and themselves that they don't see women as things. Those of you who who have been beaten down, don't give up. Trust God. Keep Him the center of your life, and keep showing your kids that God is taking care of you all.

> Train your child in the way in which you know you should have gone yourself.
>
> —Charles Spurgeon

The importance of grandparents. Grandparents today have been put on the shelf. What a tragedy! It's said that home is where the heart is. But I want to suggest something a little different for your children: Home is where the grandparents live. My advice is to live as close to one set of grandparents as possible. They can be such a vital part of child rearing. (On the other hand, many children in this day and age are being raised almost solely by grandparents because the parents are so irresponsible. As a society we're turning grandparents into parents while robbing them of their traditional roles.) Consider carefully before you trade encouragement and support from nearby grandparents for a move that will take you just one more rung up the corporate ladder.

Consistent Modeling Makes All the Difference

I've said it before, but it bears repeating: the kids are always taking notes. That's why, even more important than what we say, is how we act around our children as they're growing up. Specifically, consider these critical forms of modeling that you can practice for your kids' benefit.

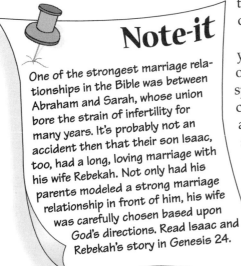

One of the strongest marriage relationships in the Bible was between Abraham and Sarah, whose union bore the strain of infertility for many years. It's probably not an accident then that their son Isaac, too, had a long, loving marriage with his wife Rebekah. Not only had his parents modeled a strong marriage relationship in front of him, his wife was carefully chosen based upon God's directions. Read Isaac and Rebekah's story in Genesis 24.

Model oneness in your marriage. If you're interested in your child's self-esteem or self-image, be on the same page with your spouse. Be shoulder to shoulder. Let no light come between you, because the children are always making mental notes about inconsistencies and conflicts in your policies with them.

And they're always looking up at you, from the earliest days. Let me give you an example. Dad comes home, finds his wife in the kitchen, gives her a little pat on the po-po. She wheels around, her lip snarled up. "Not now, the kids are watching!"

She's right; they are watching.

But imagine another scenario. The husband comes home and gives his wife a little pat on the po-po. She wheels around, exclaims, "Oh, honey! You're home." They embrace in a warm kiss.

And again the kids are watching.

From behind the children's eyes, what do they see in the first scenario? What deductions do they make about intimacy and closeness in that situation? I think you can see that the healthier of the scenes above is the second one. As husband and wife, you'll want to model that kind of closeness (because you *are* that close). What a great thing for a kid to see Mom and Dad in this light, as a couple who's committed to Christ, live by godly principles, and enjoy a satisfying intimacy in their marriage.

All I'm saying is that kids draw self-esteem from knowing Mom and Dad are on the same page. We tend to give marriage a lick and a promise, instead of the care and love God designed for it to have in order to flourish.

As you'll recall from session 3, Paul emphasized the Genesis model of marriage in Ephesians 5:28-33. That is, we are to *become one* in marriage. When you model that oneness, not only will it enhance your marriage relationship, but your kids will draw strength from it. You'll be putting people into the world who think enough of themselves not to be used or abused by other people. You'll be launching adults into society who'll likely be good husbands and good wives. So remember, kids notice how Dad treats Mom, how Mom treats Dad, how Mom treats son, and how Dad treats daughter.

Time for everyone to get up and stretch! Then have the men line up, shoulder to shoulder, and the women line up in the same way. People should be facing their spouses, standing about five feet apart. (That is, you'll have the effect of a train track of people across the room, everyone facing inward to the line across from them.)

Your leader will read aloud, one at a time, the series of bulleted questions below. You will answer by closing your eyes and taking steps either forward or backward (according to the number-scale below), depending on how close or far apart you think you and your spouse are in modeling this aspect of your relationship. After each move, stand still and open your eyes. Your leader will ask several couples to answer these questions: *Why do you think you are at this distance on this issue? What things help and/or hinder closeness for you in this area?*

Steps Forward
1 = close
2 = quite close
3 = incredibly close

Steps Backward
1 = apart
2 = far apart
3 = very far apart

- When it comes to displaying affection in front of the kids, we are . . .

- When it comes to how to discipline the children, we are . . .

- When it comes to how to use our money, we are . . .

- When it comes to deciding what to do with free time, we are . . .

- When it comes to our career choices and family goals, we are . . .

- When it comes to relating to our in-laws and relatives, we are . . .

- When it comes to our Christian beliefs and church involvement, we are . . .

Remember, kids are always making mental notes about your closeness, or lack of it. And they also take silent notice of the choices you make in life. If a twenty-eight-year-old quits her job in order to homeschool two young boys, the kids notice that. If a computer technician refuses to work overtime on weekends so he can spend more time with his girls, those kids understand. If an account executive forgoes a promotion because the move would take the family a thousand miles away from the grandparents . . . well . . . you guessed it!

Model forgiveness in your relationships. I'll be brief and let the apostle Paul do the preaching here: "Be kind and compassionate to one another, forgiving each other, just as in Christ God forgave you" (Ephesians 4:32).

We've got to model forgiveness in our marriages. Years before the apostle Paul called us to forgive one another, Jesus modeled the ultimate forgiveness as He hung on the cross, praying for those who'd condemned Him to death—all of us. Because He died for us, God forgave us. Likewise, we must model forgiveness in our families. When the time comes, we throw away the rulebooks, scrap the old record, and start fresh.

How does forgiveness actually look in real life? How do you know when you're forgiving and not just stuffing feelings? It's important for married people to explore such questions. One writer on the theme of forgiveness, Lewis Smedes, has some fantastic things to say in *Forgive and Forget.*[5] Divide into three small groups. Each group will consider one of his statements below, then answer the questions that follow.

---

1. As we forgive people, we gradually come to see the deeper truth about them, a truth our hate blinds us to, a truth we can see only when we separate them from what they did to us. When we heal our memories we are not playing games, we are not making believe. We see the truth again. For the truth about those who hurt us is that they are weak, needy, and fallible human beings. They were people before they hurt us and they are people after they hurt us.

2. You will know that forgiveness has begun *when you recall those who hurt you and feel the power to wish them well.*

3. Forgiving is tough. Excusing is easy. What a mistake it is to confuse forgiving with being mushy, soft, gutless, and oh, so understanding. Before we forgive, we stiffen our spine and we hold a person accountable. And only then, in tough-minded judgment, can we do the outrageously impossible thing: we can forgive.

■ Do you basically agree or disagree with this statement? Why?

- What personal experience with forgiveness affirms or denies what's being said here?

- If you could add one thing to this quotation, what would it be?

- Now bring the whole group together to share: What ideas in these quotations would you like to put into practice to a greater degree in your own marriage?

Model accountability as you set boundaries. Let me ask you a quick question: Do kids behave better on playgrounds *with* fences or *without* fences? They really do behave better within fenced areas, don't they? There's great value in boundaries. Kids need and appreciate guidelines. Children need large doses of vitamin N and vitamin R. The N is for "no" and the R is for "responsibility."

It's easy to snowplow the roads of life for children. It's easy to say, "Do nothing." But then we do them a disservice, because they'll become adults who know very little about self-sacrifice and self-control. And when everything has been handed to them, how could they have learned the value and satisfaction of hard work?

> There is nothing more influential in a child's life than the moral power of QUIET EXAMPLE. For children to take morality seriously they must see adults take morality seriously.
>
> —William J. Bennett

Of course, some Christians are too prone to transform themselves into Pharisees who love their strict rules and regulations. But we needn't come across as holier-than-thou about accountability and boundaries. We can wrap our rules with warmth, respect, and love. As Josh McDowell has often said: Rules without relationship lead to rebellion. How true.

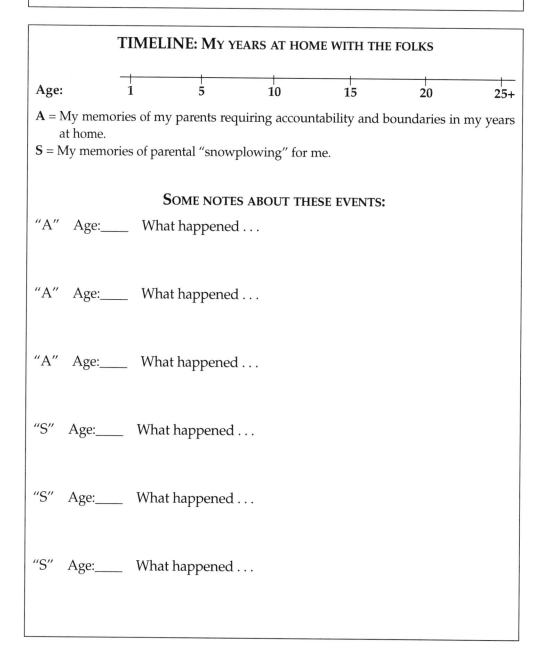

Consider how your family of origin dealt with accountability and boundaries as you were growing up. What was your parents' approach with you? Mark three "A"s on the timeline below as you recall three instances of required accountability and/or boundaries. Mark an "S" on the timeline to note memories of times when your parents seemed to "snowplow" the road ahead of you. Jot some notes about the events so you can discuss them later with a small group.

TIMELINE: My years at home with the folks

Age: 1   5   10   15   20   25+

A = My memories of my parents requiring accountability and boundaries in my years at home.

S = My memories of parental "snowplowing" for me.

SOME NOTES ABOUT THESE EVENTS:

"A"   Age:____   What happened . . .

"A"   Age:____   What happened . . .

"A"   Age:____   What happened . . .

"S"   Age:____   What happened . . .

"S"   Age:____   What happened . . .

"S"   Age:____   What happened . . .

When you've completed the timeline exercise on the previous page, gather with a small group or a partner to share your experiences of accountability and snowplowing in your original family. Then discuss the following questions together.

1. How did your parents' approach to accountability and boundary-setting affect you at the time?

2. How has their approach seemed to affect your adult functioning today?

3. How has it affected the way you do (or will) raise children?

4. In your opinion, what is the key difference between a parent who is gracious and giving and one who is a "snowplower"?

Close your session by forming a circle and holding hands. Invite everyone to spend a few moments in silence contemplating this statement: "Parents aren't perfect; just forgiven." Then the leader closes with a brief benediction.

Keeping the Promise

1. To ensure your family's success, you must put your spouse first. Look back at the two ways you planned to put your spouse first after the first session. Did you actually do these things? If so, why not plan two more ways you can *put your spouse first* in the coming weeks?

2. In two-parent homes, both spouses must play an active role. Household chores aside, how have you portioned out parenting roles in your marriage? (Consider daily tasks, such as playing with the kids, reading to them, giving them baths, leading devotionals, and so on.)

3. Decide to spend time alone with each of your children this week. Go out for an ice-cream cone, to the park, or someplace fun. Write down your plans here.

4. Look again at the "Important or Urgent" exercise in this session. Choose one activity from your Urgent list . . . and forgo it this week.

5. Try this "He Said/She Said" discussion starter: How would relieving some of the pressures of a hurried society change your family life? Do you even relish the idea of relieving some of those pressures? Or are you so used to them that life minus the frenzied pace sounds empty?

Commitment Check

Couples of Promise commit to forgiving one another and not holding grudges. They also realize how important it is to model these things in front of their children. In your journal, as a legacy to your children, write about one of your fights and tell how it was resolved. At an appropriate time, considering the children's ages, read your words to them.

For further information, consider:

Leman, Kevin, *What a Difference a Daddy Makes*, Nashville, Tenn.: Nelson, 1999.

Arterburn, Stephen and Jim Burns. *When Love Is Not Enough: Parenting Through Tough Times.* Colorado Springs, Colo.: Focus on the Family Publishing, 1992.

Sprague, Gary. *My Parents Got a Divorce.* Colorado Springs, Colo.: Kid's Hope (a ministry of the Navigators), 1992. Here's a book of letters from kids, various ages, showing how divorce has affected their lives.

Leman, Kevin. *Making Children Mind Without Losing Yours.* Grand Rapids, Mich.: Revell, 1984.

Leman, Kevin. *Becoming the Parent God Wants You to Be.* Colorado Springs, Colo.: NavPress, 1998. This is a recently published study guide—just like this one— that deals with all the topics of child raising in much more detail. Your group may want to try it when you're through with *Becoming a Couple of Promise.*

NOTES
1. David Elkind, *The Hurried Child*, rev. (Reading, Mass.: Addison-Wesley, 1988).
2. H. Norman Wright, *Always Daddy's Girl* (Ventura, Calif.: Regal, 1989), p. 10.
3. Lewis B. Smedes, *Forgive and Forget* (New York: Simon and Schuster, 1984), pp. 45,47,65-66.

Stepfamilies Don't Blend ...
They Collide!

Imagine a high-speed collision on a two-lane highway. No, not a literal crash with real cars. I'm talking about a relational pileup of devastating proportions. It's called *family blending*.

In this case, the victims are a newly married stepmom and her nineteen-year-old stepdaughter. Just days after Marge and Don got back from their honeymoon, they decided to have a few friends over for dinner. Well, Marge had moved into Don's home and she was going to make the home much more comfortable, much more intimate, and certainly much more "Martha Stewart" than it was when Dad lived in the home with his daughter and three sons.

Marge knew just how home should be and made the assumption that this house was going to be *her* home. (Note that she violated one of my basic principles, which is: "Don't move into his house; don't move into her house." If you're going to start a blended family, start on neutral turf.) Anyway, just six days after the wedding, Marge decided to have this dinner party with some of her friends. In the middle of the party, nineteen-year-old daughter Sylvia comes home and decides to make cookies for her girlfriends.

So, here's Marge, the perfectionist firstborn woman, who is under the impression that this home is *her* home. And because in her mind she has full reign of this place, she quickly sizes up her stepdaughter as intruding on her turf. She pulls the girl aside and has a little stepmother-stepdaughter talk, suggesting that there might be a better time to do the cookie thing than during this dinner party. But stubborn nineteen-year-old ignores stepmother's pleadings, makes the cookies, and creates a mess in the kitchen.

Before long, of course, there are words between Sylvia and Marge.

Not very pretty words.

To make things worse, Don sides with his daughter—largely, I think, out of guilt. He feels badly about the divorce and writes this cookie incident off as just "a little thing," telling his wife she's overreacting a bit.

Overreacting, my foot! This woman clearly sees that this is her home, her kitchen, and here's this nineteen-year-old kid coming in to mess with her stuff! Well, you can imagine what it was like. Before long, husband and wife (the newlyweds, remember, and freshly home from the honeymoon) are at each other's throats in front of the other four couples.

What fun!

To make a long story short, everyone left shortly after dinner. And a miserable time was had by all.

Stepfamilies don't blend, they collide. Nevertheless, *something* has to happen after the initial collision, right? We might as well call it a blending process, melding two different families together so they can at least try to function in peace as a single unit.

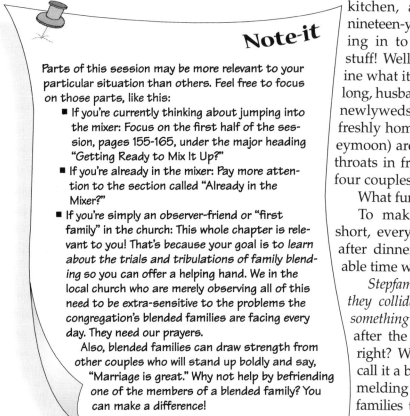

Note-it

Parts of this session may be more relevant to your particular situation than others. Feel free to focus on those parts, like this:

- If you're currently thinking about jumping into the mixer: Focus on the first half of the session, pages 155-165, under the major heading "Getting Ready to Mix It Up?"
- If you're already in the mixer: Pay more attention to the section called "Already in the Mixer?"
- If you're simply an observer-friend or "first family" in the church: This whole chapter is relevant to you! That's because your goal is to learn about the trials and tribulations of family blending so you can offer a helping hand. We in the local church who are merely observing all of this need to be extra-sensitive to the problems the congregation's blended families are facing every day. They need our prayers.

    Also, blended families can draw strength from other couples who will stand up boldly and say, "Marriage is great." Why not help by befriending one of the members of a blended family? You can make a difference!

As a supplement to this session, view "Living in a Blender" on the videotape "Keeping the Promise," Tape 2. If you wish, launch this session by playing the opening skit. Then hold a mini-debate on this resolution: "Blending two families is virtually impossible."

Getting Ready to Mix It Up?

As they continue to move forward in the process, blended families do need help. Anyone who's successfully blended a family knows that it's a terribly difficult job. Let's take a look at some of the things involved. First, consider the requirements for the initial task itself. Then I'll share some practical ways to ensure a continued, peaceful coexistence if you're already in the mixer.

So You're Thinking of Blending . . .

What does it take to blend two different households into a healthy, happy home for everyone? Consider a few time-tested guidelines:

Remember that husband and wife must blend first. There are thirteen hundred new stepfamilies every day, so the blended family is here to stay. Yet it takes about seven years to blend. The point is, you and your spouse have got to decide from the outset to be in it for the long haul—by blending first, and with the most solid of bonds.

Unfortunately, the kids will try to break up the marriage. They will try to drive a wedge between you as a couple. Part of the challenge for them is to see if you two are for real. Are you two blended? Have the two really become one? That's what those kids are trying to find out. And they're going to test you on it. Until you both blend and identifiably become that "one flesh," as the Bible describes it, the rest of the family won't blend. Surprisingly, if you remain strong, something interesting happens. When they know they can't defeat you, that you have become one in marriage, the kids begin adding wonderful things to the marriage.

If you're thinking of blending a family, go slowly, even if you think you have a prince or princess. On the next page is a little personal evaluation exercise to help you think it through. Write "yes" or "no" in the blanks provided. Jot some descriptions, as suggested. Then just spend some time thinking through your situation and your plans. Be sure you have a clear understanding of where your potential spouse is coming from—so you'll be able to blend before you attempt to blend the stepkids!

(Option: When you're through jotting your responses, go back through the items and draw a large exclamation point next to anything you've read or written that causes you concern or alarm. Determine to explore these matters further *before* you decide to move forward in the relationship.)

YES, OR NO?

____ Was your potential groom's relationship with his mom, sister, grandmother (and other women) filled with affection and respect? Describe these relationships as you've observed them so far:

____ Was your potential bride's relationships with her dad, brother, grandfather (and other men) filled with affection and respect? Describe these relationships as you've observed them so far:

____ What insights arise when you consider the quality of relationships your potential spouse had in his or her first marriage? Describe these relationships as you've observed them so far:

____ Does he or she have a temper? Jot an example that you've observed:

____ Is he or she a "controller"? Jot an example of how you know:

____ Is she or he a "defensive controller"? (Note: Defensive controllers are people who may not want to control others, but they don't want to be controlled. They're the ones who make deals with you. They're the ones who make deals with God. "Okay, God, you've got me—all ninety-four percent." It's the six percent that gets this person into trouble.)

continued

___ Is he/she tremendously exciting? (Note: A yes answer here doesn't necessarily mean it's a "go"! Don't write off Mr. Boring or Miss Bland. Look what Mr. Excitement did for you in the last marriage! This Steady Freddy might be in it for the long haul.)

___ Are you praying about this regularly? (Note: Pray. Pray that God will give you guidance. Pray long and often.) Describe the last times you prayed about this—alone and together:

___ Is the prospective partner a believer? (Note: If not, run! Run. Run, run, run. It doesn't work. You can be a champion and think you'll change all these things in his or her life, but it doesn't work. If that person truly has a heart for God, you ought to be able to see it.) Jot some notes about your potential spouse's spiritual life:

Once you decide "Yes, this is the one," stay confident that when you're united you cannot be overcome. Satan simply cannot defeat you when you stay united. Even though you are united, however, brace yourself. During the blending process, there are going to be several Armageddon evenings ahead.

Try to minimize the effect of "second time around." The so-called experts have been lying to us for years about the blended family, about remarriage, and about the second time around. Singers such as Andy Williams and the late Frank Sinatra have charmed us with songs about how love is lovelier the second time around.

Wrong! It's just not true. You've got to be smarter and wiser the second time around. It's absolutely difficult. I've mentioned the rulebooks already. You've got rulebooks based on your early life and childhood, but you've also got rulebooks based on your first marriage. Suppose in your first marriage your mate cheated on you. That's a nice, positive setup for that second marriage, isn't it? What's always going to be in the back of your mind? So when you remarry and you walk down that aisle and say those sacred vows again, ask yourself the question: How many people are getting married now? And which set of grandparents are we *not* inviting to Christmas dinner?

Read the following series of statements and decide whether they are truths or myths about the second time around. Check your responses with the answer key at the end of this chapter. Then use the statements as the basis for a discussion about the second time around.

(Note: This can be an interesting discussion for you if you are actually attempting a blended family. But it will be helpful, too, if you simply need to know more about what is involved, so you can encourage and support others.)

TRUTH OR MYTH?

____ 1. Our new family will be much like our previous families.

____ 2. It's easier to blend with older kids than with younger kids.

____ 3. An older boy will be relieved when he realizes he no longer has to be "man of the house" for newly remarried Mom.

____ 4. An older girl will probably enjoy having a new mom to serve as her role model.

____ 5. Children usually want to call their new parent "Mom" or "Dad."

____ 6. The younger kids appreciate having new sibling playmates added to their family.

____ 7. Things will go more smoothly if each parent firmly disciplines the spouse's children right from the beginning.

____ 8. When it's time for the families to merge, it's best to live in the bigger of the two adults' houses (while selling the smaller one).

____ 9. In a blended family, the teenagers are likely to wait much longer before leaving home to start their own adult lives.

____ 10. It's best to bring your potential spouse home early and often, so the kids can start getting used to him or her.

____ 11. Anger is the least likely emotion to arise when blending a family.

____ 12. Whether you respect them or not, you *do* have to love the children of your spouse.

Prepare for the special difficulties of stepparenting. While the husband-and-wife relationship is the key to blending the family, how the children are treated greatly affects the blending as well, particularly when it comes to stepparents. For now, let me just offer a word of caution to stepfathers: *The wife can love the husband only to the extent that she knows her kids are okay.*

We're talking about a mama bear and her cubs. You want to get in a tussle with a woman? Say something about her cubs, particularly that little boy cub. Stepdad, if you're going to make it in a blended family, you've got to make some changes. You can't run the family like your original, first-marriage family.

Note-it

Joseph and Mary mastered the art of blending a family. As we all know, Joseph was really just a stepdad to Jesus. Therefore, in Luke 2:41-52, when Mary and Joseph confronted Jesus in the temple to complain about His being AWOL from the family, notice who did the talking (see verse 2:48). In this case, Jesus knew what He was doing, but as marriage partners blending a family, so did Joseph and Mary.

Number off by threes using these words: "Joseph," "Mary," "Jesus." (Any gender can take any role.) Everyone will make a diary entry as one of these characters, as if they were at the end of the day following the events described in Luke 2:41-52 (read it now). The key is to talk about how Joseph, Mary, or Jesus must have felt about the conflict that had occurred.

When everyone is through jotting a diary entry, gather with the same-named group members and talk about your entries. Then discuss the three questions that follow.

DEAR DIARY. . .

What a day! After the Feast was over, there was a little confrontation in the family. Looking back, how do I feel about it? Well . . .

That about sums it up, Diary. One thing for sure, I learned that . . .

Signed, (circle one)

Joseph   Mary   Jesus

---

1. What do you think is the greatest *heartache* to be experienced by these blended family members: the dad, the mom, the kids?

   ■ Dad

   ■ Mom

   ■ Kids

2. What do you think is the greatest potential for *joy* in the lives of dad, mom, the kids?

   ■ Dad

   ■ Mom

   ■ Kids

3. Even if you've never been involved with a blended family, you have probably observed them from afar. What are your impressions regarding the difficulties involved? About the ways other "first families" can help?

   ■ Dad

   ■ Mom

   ■ Kids

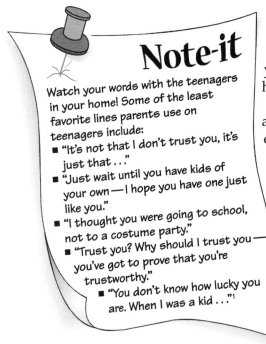

Note-it

Watch your words with the teenagers in your home! Some of the least favorite lines parents use on teenagers include:

- "It's not that I don't trust you, it's just that..."
- "Just wait until you have kids of your own—I hope you have one just like you."
- "I thought you were going to school, not to a costume party."
- "Trust you? Why should I trust you— you've got to prove that you're trustworthy."
- "You don't know how lucky you are. When I was a kid..."[1]

It Won't Be Easy!
The task of blending is so difficult that I can't stop yet with all the helpful advice! If you're trying it, here are five more things to expect and to do.

Expect anger, guilt, and jealousy. Expect it, and be prepared to deal with it. Remember that every stepfamily is born out of loss. It is born in death or divorce. All of the family members bring a chip on their shoulders to the table. Everybody has suffered a loss. Everybody is hurting. I get brave enough to suggest that stepfamilies conduct anger meetings. Because if there is ever a family that carries the anger right there on its shoulders it's the blended family. Kids, especially, need a way of voicing some of those hurts right out in the open, around the table.

The building blocks of the blended family are cemented with a mortar of anger, guilt, love, jealousy, and anger. If you're a firstborn, you noticed I used one word, *anger,* twice. On purpose. *Anger.* I used it at the beginning and at the end. Because with the pervading sense of loss comes a feeling of entitlement and anger. I want to strike out at life. If I'm seventeen years old and I want to strike out at life, whom do I strike out at? My chemistry teacher? Maybe. But it's a little easier to strike out at Mom or Stepdad.

Choose one or more of the following sets of verses to look up, working either individually or with other group members. Identify the key biblical truths that come through in each set. Then jot how those truths could apply to the development of a "well-blended family."

APPLYING SCRIPTURE TO OUR BLENDED FAMILY

On ANGER:	Key Truth	Family Application
▪ Psalm 4:4		
▪ Proverbs 15:1		
▪ Isaiah 48:9		
▪ Matthew 18:21-22		

On GUILT:	Key Truth	Family Application
▪ Psalm 103:1-14		
▪ Isaiah 43:18,25		
▪ Ezekiel 36:25-27		
▪ 1 Timothy 1:12-14		

continued

On JEALOUSY:	Key Truth	Family Application
■ 2 Corinthians 12:7-10		
■ Galatians 6:4-5		
■ Philippians 2:5-11, 4:10-13		

On LOVE:	Key Truth	Family Application
■ John 13:1-17		
■ 1 Corinthians 13:1-8		
■ 1 John 3:11-24		

Now, as a whole group, brainstorm some answers to the question that follows. Be specific and practical by suggesting even "little things" that might work. One example is already supplied for each item.

BRAINSTORM: What practical actions would help defuse anger, guilt, and jealousy? What would help infuse love in a blended family—or any family?

■ **Defusing anger:**
   (For example: Stepdad asks Mom, in private, to discipline her son about "blowing off" his chores.)

■ **Defusing guilt:**
   (For example: Mom chooses to talk with her kids about her deceased husband [the kids' "real" father] instead of always clamming up when they ask things about him.)

- **Defusing jealousy:**
  (For example: Stepdad chooses to listen and take part in conversations with his stepchildren when they talk about the deceased biological father in loving terms.)

- **Infusing love:**
  (For example: Mom and Dad let the children see them expressing affection and speaking kindly to one another, even in tense situations.)

Bring 'em home — NOT. As you enter into a relationship slowly, don't bring that potential stepparent to your home. Kids will attach very quickly to whomever you bring around your home. It's very important not to bring the kids into it *until you are thoroughly ready.* You must know *this is it.* That's when you walk the plank and do the risk-taking by bringing the kids into it.

Keep your pants on. Yes, when you date . . . please stay clothed. Sorry, but is there any better way to say it? I know it seems like such primitive advice to give to adults. But all the celebrities and so-called role models in our society today are giving us the exact opposite message. It's not wise, though. It's certainly not in keeping with biblical teaching. So, I don't care how old you are, keep your pants on.

Sell those houses! Don't plan to move into his or her house. It's the number-one mistake we make in blending families. (Remember Marge and Don!) Yes, it's the convenient, easy option, but it's also the least healthy. Sell both places and start fresh with your new family's home. The added benefit is that you can get the kids involved in the space planning and/or building.

Divide the labor. That is, prepare for well-defined responsibilities in your new family. From the beginning, realize that once you bring these two families together, the left hand will need to know what the right hand is doing. You really will have to work together and abide by a well-defined division of labor. Get ready to be more organized!

In a healthy marriage, partners take stock of their differences in temperament, interests, and abilities, and divide their roles accordingly. Sometimes this can be threatening to one or both partners, because working out their roles can result in situations that are very different from those they grew up with. It's the same with the kids, but the roles must be worked out and become clear to all involved.

In Part I below, talk about your responses with your (potential?) spouse for a moment. Then move to Part II and brainstorm together some of the practical things you could do to prevent future breakdown in areas of family life that would need to be organized and labor-divided. The first entry of Part II is already filled in as an example.

PART I

If I were to envision this (potentially?) blended family as a machine, I'd be looking at . . .

___ a massive Disgronificating Discombobulator. "With all these moving parts, I'm totally confused!"
___ a pressure-driven Seething Steamer. "Look out! She's gonna blow!"
___ a high-powered Chugging Chopper. "Stand back, or you'll get caught in those constantly whirling blades!"
___ a fairly dependable High-capacity Heater. "Let her warm up—and then be sure to give her a regular tune-up."
___ a well-oiled Master Mixer. "Just listen to that baby purr and hum along!"

Explain your response here:

PART II

- Areas of family functioning that will have to be (better) organized and/or streamlined:

- Area of Potential Breakdown: *Organizing the division of labor—"Who's going to do what around here?"*

Preventive Maintenance Procedures:
1. Idea: *Talk to the kids and find out what kinds of chores each prefers to do.*
2. Idea: *Set up a weekly "work list" so kids can see what their jobs are at a glance.*
3. Idea: *Have a weekly "check in" family meeting to discuss how things are going.*
4. Other ideas:

continued

- Area of Potential Breakdown: _____.
Preventive Maintenance Procedures:

1. Idea: _____

2. Idea: _____

3. Idea: _____

4. Idea: _____

- Area of Potential Breakdown: _____.
Preventive Maintenance Procedures:

1. Idea: _____

2. Idea: _____

3. Idea: _____

4. Idea: _____

- Area of Potential Breakdown: _____.
Preventive Maintenance Procedures:

1. Idea: _____

2. Idea: _____

3. Idea: _____

4. Idea: _____

Already in the Mixer?

So you've already jumped into the mixer. Welcome to the wonderful world of the blended family. Just remember that you don't have to be a rat, a dictatorial stepdad, or a pushover stepmother to stay in control of your stepfamily. You simply need to know that child rearing is going to look a little different in the blended family. That's because of the added issues and conflicts that come packaged with the task of making two families into one. Remember, you're starting with loss and then combining parenting styles, birth orders, family traditions, extended families, former friends . . . the list goes on and on.

"It Seemed Like a Good Idea at the Time"

Let's start with the good news. You get through blending a family, and you can do anything in life! The question to ask yourself if you're now in a blended family is: *Did I fall in love or did I fall in need?*

What do I mean? Well, imagine that you're a single parent and going it alone. All of a sudden someone walks into your life. Someone *wonderful*. What you're seeing is the relief pitcher stepping up to the mound. You see hope. You see help. You start thinking along these lines: Maybe, just maybe, we can tie up your two and my two, and that'll be six of us, and, yeah, that'll work.

If you're thinking about blending, or if you're already in the mixer, consider if your choice is (was) because of love . . . or need. In the longer blank lines below, write down all the reasons you wanted to remarry. When you're through, go back and reread your list. Try to determine if your answers stem from love or need.

In the short lines, write an "L" for love or an "N" for need. Then tally your responses and note whether there are more Ls or more Ns. Obviously, this isn't an exact science, and there will always be a mixture of love and need. So you be the judge: *Are you mostly in love or in need?*

THE REASONS THAT I WANT(ED) TO REMARRY . . .

___	_____
___	_____
___	_____
___	_____
___	_____

Then the whole scenario changes. When you were dating, the kids seemed to really like him. Within six weeks of walking down the aisle and saying "I do," however, the enemy from within begins to attack.

We have seen the enemy, and they are small. The embarrassing thing is these guys share your address. The truth is that kids within the blended family can become the archenemy to the blended family's survival and success.

A good way to nip this potential disaster in the bud is to begin practicing something I call Reality Discipline.[2] Simply put, Reality Discipline is a consistent, precise, respectful way to bring principles of respect and accountability to life, family, and marriage. You'll find its truth summed up in the Bible:

For whatsoever a man soweth, thall shall he also reap. (Galatians 6:7, KJV)

Here's how it works. Suppose your children receive a weekly allowance as members of your household. (My advice is that very young children start out receiving this money simply because they are members of your family. As they get older, they take on real responsibilities in the household.) Now suppose that your son forgets to take out the trash one day, just as my son Kevin failed to do. Because the trash bin was overflowing and really needed to be picked up the next day, I took it out for him.

"Hey, Dad, you shorted me," Kevin protested when he got his allowance that week.

"No, I didn't."

"Yes, you did, Dad! You shorted me ten dollars."

"That's because I took the garbage out for you."

"You charged me *ten dollars?*"

"Look at it this way, Kevin," I told him. "You hired a man with a doctorate to take out the garbage for you."

That's Reality Discipline.

THE TEN PRINCIPLES OF REALITY DISCIPLINE

1. The whole is always more important than the parts.
2. Have Christlike values and live by them.
3. Always put your spouse first, not the kids.
4. Balance responsibility with forgiveness and love.
5. Stick to your guns.
6. Keep responsibility where it belongs.
7. Treat people like persons, not things.
8. Use guidance, not force; action, not just words.
9. Be consistent, decisive, and respectful of your children as persons.
10. Hold your children accountable for their actions, and help them learn from experience.

How, you might be wondering, does Reality Discipline apply to adult life? As a parenting concept it seems simple enough, but what does it have to do with the rest of the family? If you think about it, you've probably already experienced the effects of Reality Discipline at some point in your life. For example:

- Put the "pedal to the metal," and you wind up paying for the right to do it in the form of a traffic fine. (Actually, I must confess that I'm a graduate of driving school!)

- Fail to pay your bills on time, and you receive strident phone calls from demanding collection agents. Continue to fail to pay and you'll find your electricity cut off, your car repossessed, or your mortgage in default.
- Be continuously late for work and be reprimanded or receive that notorious pink slip.[3]

One thing to remember is that parents, in general, tend to fall into two main categories in their approach to the kids: They are either mostly permissive or mostly authoritarian. The permissive parent usually gives in to the kids in order to keep the peace. The authoritarian parent consistently comes down too hard, without taking the time to listen and extend a little mercy.

Reality Discipline provides consequences to the actions or attitudes we take in life. Utilizing its principles will help you plan and control your life much more effectively. For dealing with kids, we might focus on Reality Discipline Principle #6 and remember it with an unpronounceable word— KRWIB ("Keep responsibility where it belongs").[4]

In the scenarios that follow, jot the Authoritarian, Reality Discipline, or Permissive approaches, whenever there is a blank. Then discuss your responses in a small group.

PERMISSIVE, AUTHORITARIAN, OR REALITY DISCIPLINE?

GETTING UP IN THE MORNING: Buford fails to get to school on time in the mornings because he stayed up late several nights in a row (watching TV) and finds it difficult to drag himself out of bed. When he asks you to write him an excuse for being tardy:

a. **Authoritarian:** You ignore his request. Instead, you make him get up two hours early, every day for a week.

b. **KRWIB:** You write a note explaining that your son overslept.

c. **Permissive:** You . . .

BEDTIME: Three-year-old Johnny takes hours to settle down at night. He's constantly calling out from his room things like "I need a drink of water" or "I have to go to the bathroom." Rarely does he settle down before midnight.

a. **Authoritarian**: You tie Johnny's door closed so he can't get out, and yell, "Don't you dare wet that bed, young man!"

continued

---

b. **KRWIB:** You . . .

c. **Permissive:** You keep getting Johnny another drink . . . and another . . . and another . . . and . . . you get the picture.

STEALING: Your five-year-old stepdaughter, Susie, takes a lollipop from the grocery store, but you don't notice until you get to the car.

a. **Authoritarian:** You go back in the store and announce in a loud voice: "Attention, everyone! My daughter is a thief!" You then storm out of the store, promising Susie a huge spanking at home.

b. **KRWIB:** You take her back in the store, apologize to the clerk, and pay for the candy. Then you throw it away. (Don't want to reward little Susie for stealing!)

c. **Permissive:** You . . .

TALKING BACK: Zelda, eight years old, has gotten vocally abusive about the choices of clothes she's been given to wear to a party. She's just hollered, "Oh, shut up! You're not even my real mom!" Your response is . . .

a. **Authoritarian:** You . . .

b. **KRWIB:** You leave the room for a minute to control your anger. Then you come back in and say, "I know I'm not your real mom, but we have to learn to respect one another anyway. Furthermore, I do not appreciate this kind of behavior and will not tolerate it." If the behavior doesn't change, you say: "I see you are choosing not to go to the party."

c. **Permissive:** You cringe and say, "Come on, Zelda! You're hurting my feelings! I know I haven't done a very good job lately. I'm sorry."

FIGHTING/SIBLING RIVALRY: Buddy and Betsy, stepsiblings, are six and eight years old. As the family is watching a TV program together, Buddy decides to pester Betsy by poking her. The first time he creates a disturbance . . .

a. **Authoritarian:** You yell, "Quit it, or I'll tan your hide!" Later, you throw pillows and other objects at the persistent Buddy.

b. **KRWIB:** You take him aside and say, "Buddy, you have a choice. You can sit quietly and watch the program with us or you can leave the room. You decide." If Buddy persists, you take action—firmly but gently removing Buddy to his room for a stipulated amount of time. At that time, you tell him he may return when he is ready.

c. **Permissive:** You . . .

continued

HOMEWORK: Ninth-grader Johnny fritters away his study-hall time at school and then procrastinates at home until the last minute. Eventually it's "crisis time," because homework is unfinished when it's time to go to bed.

a. **Authoritarian:** You lock all of Johnny's schoolbooks in a drawer and yell, "Okay, if that's what you want, then you're not going to do any homework for the next two weeks. I don't care if you get straight Fs for the quarter! See how you like that!"

b. **KRWIB:** You . . .

c. **Permissive:** You do Johnny's homework for him because you are very concerned for him and want him to get good grades. (After all, suppose he were to blow his chances for college!)

TEEN DATING: Fourteen-year-old Trisha is very mature and physically developed for her age. She wants to date a boy who is three years older. She has never officially dated before.

a. **Authoritarian:** You . . .

b. **KRWIB:** You say, "Honey, you may not want to hear this, but your mother and I agree that you can't go on single dates at fourteen, particularly with a boy who is three years older. We think that sixteen is a much more realistic age to start single dating."

Your daughter protests that you don't trust her, she's not that kind of girl, he's not that kind of boy, and so on. You then tell her, "Honey, we believe you and we trust you. We also have the responsibility not to let you get into situations that put you at risk."

c. **Permissive:** You say, "Great! When can we meet your new-found love!"

Let me illustrate further. I learned years ago as a young dean of students in charge of discipline at a university that Reality Discipline can apply to almost any situation. I had to administer what was called the code of conduct, but some of the most difficult conflicts to deal with occurred among the office staff. One particular secretary used to come to my office and regale me with her complaints about another secretary's job performance. I eventually learned, instead of listening like the village idiot to her complain for forty minutes, to say, "I'm glad you brought this to my attention." Then I took her to the other woman's desk.

"Alice, Mary Lou has something she wants to tell you," I announced.

Suddenly Mary Lou's complaint had diminished. "Oh, it's nothing really important," she stammered out. "When are you going to be through using the copy machine?"

I've learned in my business life that if you have one person complaining about another, it's best to bring them together and say, "This person has something to say," and let them thrash it out. It cuts through the psychological maneuvering of a conflict and the chaos that can result. It keeps responsibility where it belongs. When I simply listened to Mary Lou's problems, I wasn't really helping her or myself. She may have felt better for airing her grievances, but I felt like a trash bucket. And the problem was not solved. By talking directly to Alice, Mary Lou had a chance of resolving her differences with her.[5]

If you've already blended, consider these final suggestions as overall guidelines for all family members to understand and heed.

Don't try to go back. It may not be perfect, but this is the hand you've been dealt in life. You can't go back. You can't go back to the original marriage. The family will never be the same.

Don't make triangles. Realize that your ex-spouse can throw a grenade into your living room tonight

simply by picking up the phone and dialing your number. The whole family can be thrown off by a phone call. Suppose, for example, your ex-spouse calls and tells you, "Have the children ready. I'm taking them fishing." Then he doesn't show. If you get in touch with your feelings, what do you feel like doing? That doesn't help. What should you say? "I don't know where your dad is. But you know his number. Give him a call."

That's how you avoid triangulation: You keep the lines of relationships where they belong.

Don't pontificate. Or to put it another way: Don't go around dropping verbal bombshells. Avoid issuing unilateral pronouncements. Don't make decisions that will affect the family without checking with the family. This goes back to your style of leadership. If you're a man and you're strong willed and all that, you think nothing of pontificating. "I'm the man. I'm gonna make the decisions." In a blended family, that's suicide. You might as well take your shoe off and kick yourself in the teeth, because it's about as useful. This is basic but essential advice. Realize that you're throwing kids together who don't have a real relationship except the one you've created. They're living with strangers.

Do keep everyone involved. Another way to say this is "Everybody helps." Your home is not a hotel. No one just comes and goes. Everybody pitches in, and every family member has jobs to do. We rob self-esteem from children when we fail to hold them accountable and don't give them the opportunity to give back to the family.

Do keep listening—to everybody. The key is to remember that no one member of the family is more important than the family as a whole. This is one of those principles from Reality Discipline. It becomes even more important in a blended family. Yet everyone's individuality is important; guard it, and take time to listen, listen, listen.

Do discipline your own children first. If your spouse is gone and you're in charge, obviously you have to act on things. But whenever possible, let each parent discipline his own child. Instead of starting with drill-sergeant-like discipline, work instead on forming a relationship with your stepchildren over a period of time. Defer to the parent of your stepchild. Don't treat kids the same because, just as God made you and your spouse to be different, God made them different.

Remember: *You don't have to love the other kids. You do have to respect them.* Love does not demand its own way. A mother told me that once she started to respect her husband's children, she soon discovered that she had learned to love them as well.

Do pray and worship together. This will strengthen your marriage and blend your family with a spiritual dimension that ultimately permeates everything else you do.

Note-it

A word about spanking: I believe there are times when a spanking is an appropriate response, but it rarely should be the first response. Here are some things to consider:

- If you've tried some form of Reality Discipline, and the child is still willfully disobedient, then a spanking may be in order.
- Consider the age of the child. Spanking is appropriate only for children ages two to seven.
- Spanking should consist only of a couple swats to the bottom — with a hand only — followed by holding the child and assuring him or her of your love.
- Use a private place; no public humiliation of your child!
- Don't spank when you're angry. It's to be a thoughtful action, not a hot-headed reaction. (Note: Never spank if you were abused as a child.) No child is going to be harmed by an occasional spanking that follows the guidelines above.

However, if you find you are spanking every day, back off and reevaluate the situation. Are your children getting lots of love, acceptance, and encouragement? Get professional counseling if needed.[7]

Take the following mini-quiz to determine how well you're blending so far. There's an answer key at the end of this session.

ARE YOU MIXED UP?

1. You're in a rush to get ready for work and your hairbrush is missing from its place. You:
    a. borrow your stepdaughter's, assuming that she took yours.
    b. stop and buy a new one on the way to work.
2. Your friend is selling tickets for the theater at a bargain price. You:
    a. buy tickets for the whole family so you can have a family night out.
    b. check to see if anyone else is interested first.
3. Your stepson asks you to call his father and explain why he wants to miss their weekend together to attend your daughter's baptismal service. You:
    a. get on the phone and use the opportunity to witness to your stepson's father.
    b. encourage your stepson to witness to his father himself and arrange to have the baptismal date changed if necessary.
4. Your stepfamily can't find a new home in your son's old school district. Moving would be yet another loss for him. You decide to:
    a. stay in your old home temporarily until something becomes available.
    b. explain to your son that you're starting a new life, including a new home and school, and starting fresh will benefit everybody.
5. Your stepdaughter is with you only on weekends when you have family work days. You:
    a. let her watch TV while everyone is cleaning their rooms.
    b. give her responsibility, such as helping prepare lunch for the family.

To close this session, consider laying hands on those who express need. Focus on each person's situation as others take turns praying aloud.

Keeping the Promise

1. Take your stepchild on an outing by yourself.

2. Consider holding an Anger Meeting, where everyone gets their problems off their chests by taking turns presenting "I" statements about how they are feeling.

3. Pray with your family for your family during a daily or weekly devotional time. Keep it brief and try to work it into your family life naturally so a regular pattern can be established.

4. If you are not in a blended family yourself, try being an encouragement to someone who is. Ask the Lord for wisdom in deciding who to befriend. Write down that person's name, address, and telephone number on the next page:

Name:
Address:
Telephone:

5. Try this "He Said/She Said" discussion starter: How can Christian families hold up the "ideal" of marriage while dealing with the "real" of divorce?

Commitment Check

Couples of Promise support one another's spiritual growth to the benefit of the entire family. Did you help your spouse get the most out of this study by your willing participation? Are there any sections or chapters you need to review together?

Answer key to "Truth or Myth?" exercise on page 158:

They are all myths! (Note: With regard to number 1, remember that you cannot replicate your original family, even if it was a great one. Regarding number 2: In fact, a lot of older kids *resent* the fact Mom or Dad would even think about remarriage.)

Answer key to "Are You Mixed Up?" on page 173:

If you answered "b" on every question, you're well on your way to blending. If not, try rereading the practical guidelines provided in this chapter.

For further information, consider:

Townsend, John. *Hiding from Love*. Colorado Springs, Colo.: NavPress, 1991. See especially the chapter titled "Harmful Hiding: Six Critical Stages," starting on page 147.

Leman, Kevin. *Becoming the Parent God Wants You to Be*. Colorado Springs, Colo.: NavPress, 1998.

Leman, Kevin. *What a Difference a Daddy Makes*. Nashville, Tenn.: Nelson, 1999.

NOTES
1. Adapted from Kevin Leman, *Keeping Your Family Together . . .*, p. 255.
2. This section on Reality Discipline is adapted from material in Kevin Leman, *Living in a Stepfamily . . .*, pp. 36-38.
3. Leman, *Keeping Your Family Together . . .*, p. 23.
4. This exercise is adapted from Kevin Leman, *Becoming the Parent God Wants You to Be*, beginning on p. 184.
5. Leman, *Keeping Your Family Together . . .*, pp. 76-79.
6. This summary is adapted from *Becoming the Parent God Wants You to Be*, beginning on p. 74.
7. Adapted from *Becoming the Parent God Wants You to Be*, p. 189.

IMPROVE YOUR MARRIAGE AND FAMILY.

Becoming the Parent God Wants You to Be

Written by best-selling author Dr. Kevin Leman,
Becoming the Parent God Wants You to Be is a real-life
parenting curriculum that helps you discover that you can
be a great parent—without being perfect!

Becoming the Parent God Wants You to Be
(Kevin Leman) $12

201 Great Questions for Married Couples

Whether you've been married five or fifty years,
this creative communication tool will enhance your relationship.
Useful for both couples and groups.

201 Great Questions for Married Couples
(Jerry D. Jones) $6

201 Great Questions for Parents and Children

This easy-to-use tool helps you interact with your children
to build mutual understanding and deeper family relationships
as you discuss differing perspectives and problems.

201 Great Questions for Parents and Children
(Jerry D. Jones) $6